CONTENTS

THE PLANT LOVER'S GUIDE TO DAHLIAS

ANDY VERNON

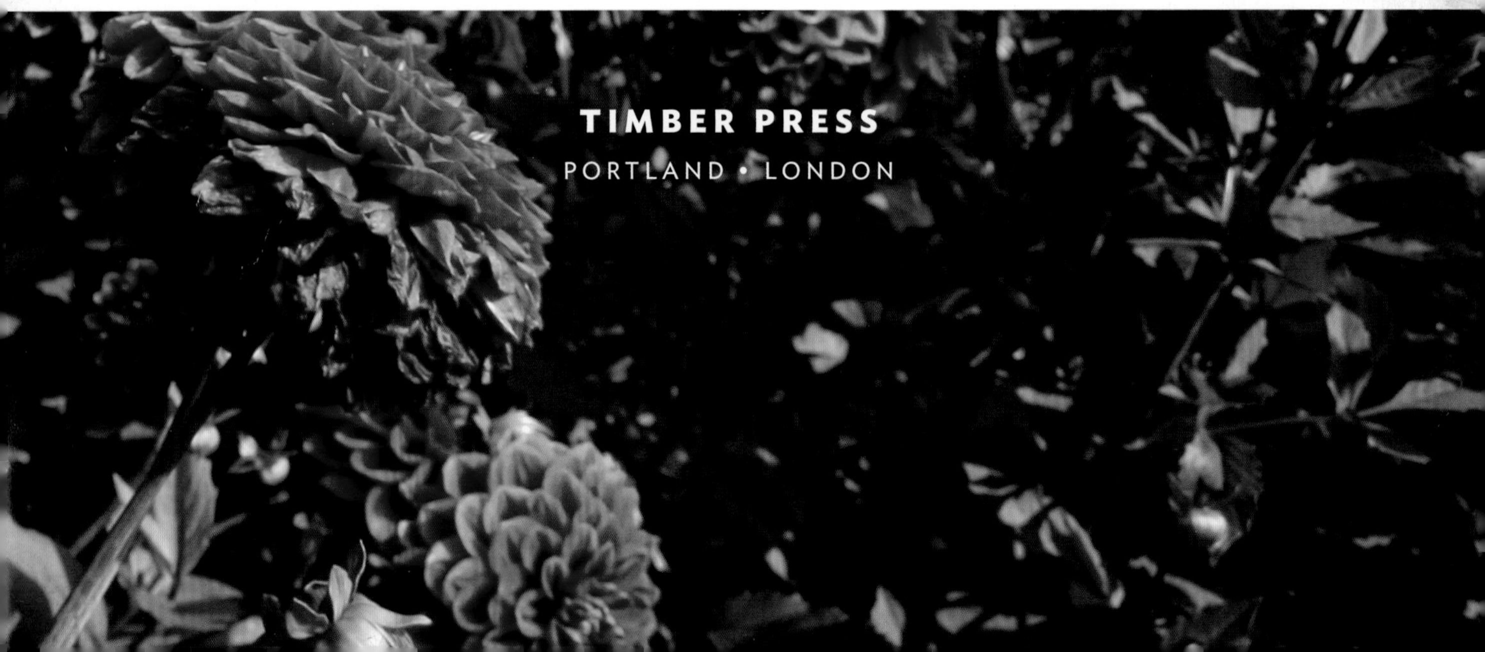

TIMBER PRESS
PORTLAND • LONDON

THE
PLANT LOVER'S GUIDE
TO
DAHLIAS

WHY I LOVE DAHLIAS

I think it's important we get this right from the start. I don't just like dahlias: **I love them.**

They are totally wonderful and fabulously gorgeous. There's something about dahlias I just can't resist, and it's a lot more than their incredible range of colours and forms.

Dahlias are like no other flower. They are the most variable and incredible characters, with larger-than-life personalities: from big, vibrant, bodacious bloomers with a full knicker-box of petals to delicate, daisy-like damsels to devilishly dark velvet varieties—and let's not forget some of the most eccentrically shaped and crazy clown-coloured cultivars. In late summer, when they're standing in the sun and flaunting their flowers, they are having the most wonderful time. They brighten my day, make me smile, and hug my soul.

For a long while, the gardening good-taste brigade considered dahlias rather too much, or a bit common. Now, at long last, a dahlia revival is occurring, and a resurgence of interest in these dazzling blooms is well under way. They are the comeback queens of the herbaceous border, and are being welcomed into our gardens to inject drama, courageous colour, and some late-summer fireworks.

I feel like I have been waiting quite some time for this new dahlia craze to catch on. In 1998 I attended the Royal Horticultural Society Hampton Court Flower Show and fell completely in love with a small exhibit by Winchester Growers, which then held the National Collection of Dahlias. I remember thinking, why aren't more people growing these incredible plants?

Many gardeners, growers, breeders, and aficionados across the dahlia world are playing an important role in the new dahlia revolution. In the United Kingdom, certain pivotal individuals stand out. We have much for which to thank the late Christopher Lloyd and *Dahlia* 'Bishop of Llandaff'. In his iconic garden at Great Dixter, Lloyd and his head gardener, Fergus Garrett, set the British horticultural world alight. They developed an incredible exotic garden where once a formal rose parterre had stood. The garden features huge, leafy, sub-tropical–style planting and rich, dramatic, herbaceous perennials and annuals. It became a huge, much-talked-about hit.

Of the many dahlia varieties grown and championed at Dixter, 'Bishop of Llandaff' was the first to be universally accepted into polite gardening circles. It became very popular in exotic planting schemes and mixed borders in the 1990s. While complementing red hot pokers, cannas, crocosmias, and heleniums, its deep black divided leaflets and rich red flowers also contrasted brilliantly with acid green foliage and giant leaves and fronds.

Dahlia 'Bishop Of Llandaff' complements cannas at Kings Heath Park.

In some ways 'Bishop of Llandaff' is a most un-dahlia-like dahlia, as it is compact, bushy, and almost black, with divided foliage and clean, simple flowers. It didn't cause too much curtain twitching or ruffle too many feathers, and it sat well among the accepted perennial favourites of the time. 'Bishop of Llandaff' was first raised in the 1920s, so it is a relatively old variety, but around 60 years later—and for the next two decades—it was to become terribly in vogue and would eventually pave the way for a new fashion for smaller single and semi-double flowered dahlias, as well as dark-leaved varieties.

Not far away in East Sussex, another dahlia guru began developing a passion for dahlias. Sarah Raven uncovered wonderful new varieties and re-discovered some classics that were perfect for cutting. I was lucky enough to get to know her when I worked with her on various BBC television gardening series. We soon discovered a shared love for these plants. Sarah has done much to champion vibrant dahlia varieties in rich single colours, and she has a passion for the deepest, darkest crimson and claret types. Her eye for colour and flower form is second to none, and she's done a great deal to encourage a much bolder use of colour throughout our gardens.

Since about 2003, down in deepest Cornwall at the National Collection of Dahlias, Michael Mann, Jon Wheatley, and Mark Twyning have done sterling work to bring dahlias to a new audience. They have staged the most astounding dahlia displays at Royal Horticultural Society flower shows across the United Kingdom, often bringing plants into bloom months in advance at the Chelsea Flower Show. Mark Twyning has blazed a trail by breeding the most exciting new garden varieties. These plants are relatively small and compact, with simple single and semi-double flowers. His varieties are now some of the most popular garden dahlias in the United Kingdom. Across Europe and further afield, we are experiencing a new wave of breeding smaller, more compact varieties, perfect for domestic gardens and containers.

Dahlia lover may seem like a strange term, but I like it best. I am not an exhibition or professional grower. I hugely admire men and women who can grow the blooms to complete perfection, and I appreciate the passion that ignites their quest for these ultimate blooms. But I just want lots and lots of dazzling blooms, in as many different colours and varieties as I can pack into my patch. The challenge of growing and integrating good garden varieties into quite a small suburban space is what really excites me.

In recent years I've loved growing dahlias in all sorts of pots and containers and discovering with which herbaceous plants they look good and grow well. I'm addicted to strong, vibrant colours, particularly in late summer, when the light is getting slightly lower but the evenings are still long and warm. The summer garden spectacle is reaching its absolute peak, and this is the dahlias' time.

Dahlias have true international appeal. They are loved and adored all over the world in an incredible number of countries: Germany, France, Japan, the Netherlands, New Zealand, the United Kingdom, and the United States. My latest obsession is watching dahlia videos, made by passionate growers from around the world, on social networking sites. I love to study the ways in which different dahlia growers do things. Everyone has their own methods and tips, but no matter what the approach, these short films show that growing dahlias for garden display is easy no matter where you live.

Dahlia exhibitors have made the care, cultivation, and display of the plants into an art and science. This is necessary when you require absolute perfection. However, if, like me, you're really just a very keen gardener with

Dahlia 'Royal Visit' is a charming purple-and-white blended variety.

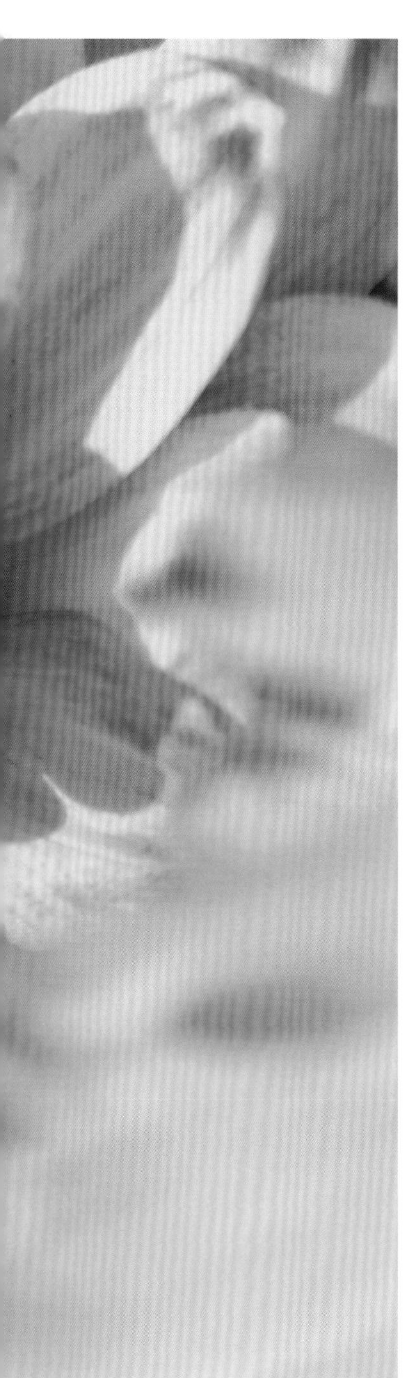

Dahlia 'Mrs McDonald Quill'. A large and dramatic bicoloured decorative.

a healthy love of all things colourful and floral, you will find that dahlias are such easy plants to grow in the garden.

I love propagating dahlias, growing them, collecting new varieties, and giving friends excess plants I've grown from seed. My partner refuses to cull a seedling, so fastidious pricking out and potting on results in a lot of excess plants to give away. I love putting together simple, colourful bunches of cut blooms, or placing individual blooms in separate jam jars or vases to create a mini dahlia display in a window ledge. Most of all, I love to explore how dahlias can be grown with other garden plants as well as single specimens in containers.

If you're lucky enough to live in a climate with dry, mild winters, you may find that you can leave your dahlia tubers in the ground over winter with just a simple layer of mulch. The plants will then return the following year, often bigger and better than before. What could be easier?

Times have changed, and dahlias are being re-invented for more modern gardens and tastes. Right now, it seems that the most amazing dahlia varieties are being bred around the world specifically for characteristics not previously explored in such depth, such as interesting leaf forms; new and re-discovered flower forms; deeper, richer colours; compact varieties for container growing; and single, scented, and star-shaped versions. I want to share my passion for these flowers and pass on my tips from years of garden growing. I've had my fair share of dahlia disasters so I hope I can help you avoid some of my mishaps and succeed the first time around.

Dahlias have been done a great disservice over the years. They've been branded old-fashioned, fussy, hard work, and uncool. Not so. These are great plants with great personalities, and it's time to set the record straight. It really is an exciting time to discover these plants.

DESIGNING WITH FLAMBOYANT FLOWERS

Dahlias are bushy, herbaceous perennials. They grow from tubers and form a substantial, leafy plant that flowers for months. Growing them in the garden is a very different experience than raising other summer-flowering bulbs or corms. Designing with dahlias is about creating a floral picture that has impact and drama that sustains and matures across the whole summer season. Unlike lilies or gladioli, dahlias don't just pop up, give you a week of glorious flower spikes festooned with blooms, and gracefully disappear. Dahlia planting combinations make a scene that lasts all summer and well into autumn.

Dahlias come in all shapes and sizes, from tiny munchkin plants that are only 15 cm (6 in.) tall to giant-leaved, bamboo-stemmed tree dahlias that grow several metres in height, and everything in between. There are so many different ways to grow them in the garden: in window boxes and containers on balconies and patios; among all sorts of grasses, herbaceous perennials, and shrubs in mixed borders; on their own in a dedicated bed for display or cutting; among exotic and architectural plants to create a sub-tropical scheme; and with other highly floriferous bedding plants to make a sea of non-stop colour. Giant decorative dahlias, if given some decent support and grown along a boundary, will also create a quick and impressive temporary hedge. Dahlias are ideal for experimenting with and having fun. They will bring joy to your garden.

An amazing display by Bournemouth City Council at the Royal Horticultural Society's Hampton Court Palace Flower Show showcased a range of white dahlia varieties with umbellifers, and also white and lime green snapdragons, cosmos, nicotiana, and nigella.

Herbaceous Beds and Borders

No mixed herbaceous border is complete without a bold injection of dahlia razzamatazz somewhere along its length. During the summer months I love to visit grand stately homes, parks, nurseries, and private gardens to collect ideas and inspiration for my own tiny end terrace. I have been lucky enough to visit some of the very best, but I classify those without any sort of dahlia drama or display as "close, but no cigar."

There are some common themes in the gardens where dahlias are used to best effect. Dahlias either represent the strong central colour theme of a bed or border at that particular point, or dramatically contrast with the dominant hue and inject some excitement and energy. Either way, dahlias are planted with courage. These are bold groups, usually of three plants, and often a particular colour or form is repeated to add rhythm.

You can cherry-pick from all the different groups of dahlias when choosing those best suited to growing in containers, mixed herbaceous borders, and plantings in the garden. However, the slightly less complex, less formal-looking flower types feel more at home among other plants. These more gardenesque dahlias are the simple, slightly looser, more unusual, and less perfect flower forms. I tend to favour simple, daisy-like single forms and collerettes, which have a ruffle of tiny petaloids around their central disc of florets. Bees and butterflies adore these too. I also love to use semi-double and peony blooms with their fuller rows of voluptuous petals, and star or single orchid types with their pointy, wavy, windmill flowers. The larger, looser cactus and semi-cactus types also look amazing in the border, especially the very shaggy, tousled, almost untidy-looking varieties. Add to these a few kooky powder puff anemone types here and there to spice things up nicely.

Formal decoratives, ball, and pompon dahlias are great fun, but I think these more precise, conventional dahlia forms look better in bedding displays, traditional mixed borders, and cut flower beds. To my eyes, the tight formality of these types of blooms doesn't always sit well among drifts of herbaceous perennials and grasses in more contemporary, naturalistic perennial planting schemes.

When it comes to picking a great variety of dahlia for your garden, you need to consider the type or form of dahlia, the colour of the bloom and foliage, and the plant's overall habit and stature. These factors often determine whether it will work well among your other garden plants. If your colour choice contrasts or harmonizes well with your planting scheme, if the form of dahlia adds extra interest among your other shaped blooms, and if your plant's habit adds a slightly different silhouette, you're probably on the right track.

With so many flower forms and recognized groups, it is fun to have many diverse types of dahlias in different situations across the garden planted in confident groups. The beauty of these incredible plants lies in their variety. If you want a coherent and well-designed display, be careful not to have just one plant of a variety here and there. A strong grouping of just one cultivar is much more effective. Alternatively, plant a mixed group of carefully chosen flower forms in tints, tones, and shades of one hue. One of everything, in a kaleidoscope of colours, can look a bit too much as if the dahlia circus has come to town—even for me, and I love eccentricity.

Many good garden dahlias require little to no staking. 'Bishop of Llandaff', 'Bishop of York', and 'David Howard' are three classic examples. Some of the larger, more dramatic varieties are going to need supporting, so get this in place good and early, ideally right after planting and no later than when the young growth reaches 25 cm (10 in.).

Don't be under any illusions when planting dahlias. Most varieties don't really want to play nicely with others. They want to show off, outshine, and flower as flamboyantly as possible. Think carefully when picking herbaceous border companions for dahlias. Too many other plants with big, colourful, attention-grabbing blooms can fight and spoil the overall effect. Plants with very different flower structures, leaf forms, and textures, as well as those of a contrasting height and habit, can help create a fantastic, multi-textured display.

Dahlias look amazing among a vast range of other plants. Don't be shy. Bring out the big guns: large and luscious architectural foliage, grasses, herbaceous perennials galore, half-hardy annuals, tropical climbers, and tender, exotic-looking houseplants. All should be encouraged to join in the dahlia fun throughout the summer.

Two UK locations with incredibly rich, exhilarating planting associations are Great Dixter House and Gardens in East Sussex, and Cotswold Garden Flowers in Worcestershire. Both do a beautiful job of using dahlia varieties in mixed plantings and with unusual choice varieties of herbaceous perennials. Be sure to visit both if the opportunity arises.

At Great Dixter, dahlias are also combined in creative, sometimes experimental, ways in mixed herbaceous borders and informal plantings throughout different areas of the garden. Strong, contrasting, and occasionally clashing colours are placed among myriad foliage textures and shapes. I always leave feeling invigorated and eager to try new planting combinations at home. I have yet to find another garden that uses dahlias in such a refreshing and challenging manner.

Wandering through the beds and borders at Cotswold Garden Flowers has likewise inspired many of my dahlia plantings. Shimmering field grass and euphorbia foliage behind a ravishingly red *Dahlia* 'Murdoch' at the nursery first motivated me to try planting grasses with dahlias.

Deepest cherry pink *Dahlia* 'Hillcrest Royal' with yellow crocosmias and blue salvias at Great Dixter.

At my favourite local nursery, Cotswold Garden Flowers, this simple planting combination of decorative dark-leaved *Dahlia* 'Hot Chocolate' with *Macleaya cordata* in the background works brilliantly well. The shape and form of the two plants are such a strong contrast, and the smoky-soft colours of the plume poppy help to set off the dark foliage and flowers of the dahlia.

Exotic or Sub-Tropical Plantings

It has become a well-established practice to use dahlias to add glamorous splashes of colour in exotic or sub-tropical–style planting schemes, as they are the perfect complement to architectural and giant, jungle-like foliage. Christopher Lloyd's garden at Great Dixter ignited a new trend for using dahlias in the garden. Christopher proved just how brilliantly dahlias could be used to full effect in all sorts of situations, and Fergus Garrett now continues his passion and pioneering ethos.

At one place in the garden, *Dahlia* 'David Howard' and *Verbena bonariensis* jostle for position underneath towering spires of *Arundo donax* var. *versicolor*. Elsewhere in the exotic garden, an impressive row of large pink decorative *D.* 'Emory Paul' grows alongside the yew hedge, lending a wonderful *Day of the Dahlias* atmosphere to this corner of the garden.

The incredible jungle atmosphere in the exotic garden at Great Dixter is intensified by the generous and bold plantings of dahlia varieties like *Dahlia coccinea* 'Mary Keen' and layer upon layer of lush architectural plants like dog fennel, Chinese rice-paper plant, and Japanese banana.

Containers

Container plantings with dahlias can be eye-catching, elegant, and contemporary. They can also provide perfect focal points around the garden and enhance paved patio areas and decking. In recent years, many new dahlias have been bred with a more compact habit and great foliage. These are shorter than the more traditional varieties and intended especially for containers, so they have opened up fresh opportunities for tiny gardens and balconies. They require much less or no staking, and some can hold their flowers upright so viewers can fully appreciate them from above.

There are various series of dahlias to look out for: Classic, Dark Angel, Gallery, Happy Days, Happy Single, Labella Piccolo, Melody, and Mystic are just a few in an ever-expanding list. Some have been developed for their low-growing and branching habit, some for their early and prolific flowering period, and some for their black

Dahlia 'Sweetheart' is just one of a number of dwarf single varieties perfect for planting in small pots.

Dahliettas

IN RECENT YEARS I have seen many new, ultra small varieties of *Dahlia*, often labelled "Dahlietta," used in bedding schemes and as container plants. These naturally compact mini dahlias reach a height of only 15 to 20 cm (6–8 in.). I have really warmed to them. I will always be a big-blooming, tall dahlia fanatic at heart, but these tiny types are great fun and they serve a purpose. Now we can all enjoy dahlias in the smallest of window boxes, in really small individual pots and containers, in hanging baskets, in woolly planting pockets, and even as temporary houseplants or table centres in a sunny location indoors. They really are perfect little poppet-size plants.

foliage, vivid blooms, and self-supporting nature. Others are favoured for their tiny stature.

When growing dahlias in containers, you don't have to limit yourself to the more dwarf or compact varieties. If the pot is big enough and you don't mind plenty of watering and feeding throughout the summer (an automatic leaky hose watering system makes life so much easier), you can grow any dahlia you like. Avoid very lofty cultivars, however. They will be a bit taller in a large pot, so the flowers may feel too high up to appreciate fully.

It is critical, when planting in containers, to use rich, high-quality, free-draining multi-purpose compost. I always choose a heavy, loam-based formula. I've found that peat- and coir-based composts dry out far too quickly in hot summers, and they can be difficult to quickly and thoroughly re-wet. The weight of loam also provides extra stability in windy situations. I recommend incorporating water-retaining crystals or gel, just like what you might use when planting a hanging basket. A dahlia that dries out at the roots on a regular basis won't flower well, so it's key to make sure the roots are well hydrated.

Always have a snug-fitting drip tray underneath your containers. Water should run through the pot, but the excess should be taken up by capillary action right after watering so the roots grow strong and head down toward the base of the container. Good drainage is also vital, however. No dahlia likes to sit in saturated, waterlogged conditions for a long time, so be sure to empty out drip trays regularly.

In a container, dahlia foliage is that much more visible, so it is even more essential to grow the plants well to ensure the leaves are glossy and healthy. Feeding is paramount. A pot has much less soil for the roots to access, and the much smaller volume of compost needs to work harder to supply the plant with all the nutrients it needs throughout the growing season. At planting time it is important to incorporate slow-release fertilizers that degrade slowly, such as hoof and horn meal and bonemeal, or specialist inorganic granules. In the height of summer and well into the autumn, be sure to water the container regularly with diluted organic tomato fertilizer or a high-potash liquid fertilizer. This will ensure good flowering for as long as possible. Dahlias planted in containers can wilt, even though you might be watering them regularly. If this happens, move them to a location with less afternoon sun to keep them from overheating. But do not allow plants to dry out completely, which will affect their flowering potential and cause the lower foliage to start dying off prematurely.

I enjoy making mixed container plantings with dahlias. There is quite an art to choosing the right companions in a container, but the key qualities are contrasting habit, good foliage, and great flowers. I choose the dahlia first. I often pick a variety from the Classic, Mystic, Happy Single, Happy Days, or Dark Angel series. My favourite small dahlias for containers are the dark-leaved varieties. The contrast between flower and foliage is just

Dahlia 'Melody Gipsy' is one of the brilliant Melody series. Compact, floriferous plants have all the attitude and appeal of much larger varieties.

that much stronger, and silver, burgundy, and lime green leaves work so well with them. There are good container dahlias with plain green foliage, but many of them work best grown alone or as a group of plants of the same variety in a very large pot.

A number of other dark-leaved dwarf varieties are exceptionally good choices for containers, and well worth hunting for if delicious, dark foliage is your thing. *Dahlia* 'Dannevirke', a rich, cherry pink single with a dark central eye, is great for containers. At the tips of each of its petals the pink blends into a pale shade of cotton candy. The bees go absolutely mad for it in my garden. Another handsome and floriferous container plant is *D.* 'Gallery Art Nouveau', a compact variety with good deep green, rather than bronze, foliage.

Plants in the Melody series of container dahlias have a flowering height between 50 and 75 cm (20–30 in.). They range from ball and decorative types to waterlily and semi-cactus forms. They are compact and robust, and in some ways they have the attitude of a big flowering dahlia on a much shorter plant.

Other impressive container varieties I discovered at the Royal Horticultural Society's trial include *D.* 'Rojo Paramo', a ravishing raspberry decorative and part of the XXL Aztec series. This dahlia collection consists of a wide assortment of varieties with large, fully double, decorative flowers on very short, stocky plants. *Dahlia* 'My-nute Blend' is

Dahlia 'My-nute Blend' is floriferous and has lovely straight, long stems. This perfect container dahlia is good for cutting too.

Dahlia 'Rojo Paramo' is one of the large-flowering but dwarf XXL Aztec range. A great range of colours is available, but the deep shades are my favourites. Look for deep red 'Alamos', burgundy 'Taxco', and purple 'Puebla'.

also impressive; it has very prolific double orange and yellow blooms with straight stems holding the flowers high above the foliage. It is a good container, cut-flower variety.

Impression is a great series with a range of short and compact collerette-type dahlias. They are fun to grow and popular with pollinating insects. I'm a fan of many of these new compact types of container dahlias for small gardens, balconies, and window boxes. (A lot of brand-new varieties and series are appearing all the time. It's rather hard to keep up!) I like experimenting with the larger garden varieties too. When grown well in large pots among interesting planting combinations, all sorts of dahlias can thrive and put on a fabulous display in a container.

If you decide to grow a medium or large garden dahlia variety in a container, plant plenty of colourful bedding or interesting foliage plants around the edge. These will help hide any untidy basal foliage that you may want to remove as the dahlia matures. You almost need to design a skirt or screen of plants for the understory, using plants in colours that contrast or complement the colour of the dahlia flower and foliage. There is nothing worse than a pot holding a big dahlia with naked knobbly stems, where all the flowers and foliage look good from only about halfway up the display. Choose hardworking bedding plants that are also slightly shade tolerant, such as petunias, calibrachoas, and impatiens. These are all great at providing extra flower interest. Or pick foliage plants like coleus, heuchera, foam flowers, heucherella, ornamental clovers, and *Bidens ferulifolia* 'Goldeneye' for foliage texture and interest. Be adventurous. There are so many plants that will make amazing combinations.

Dahlias grow vigorously, so in any mixed container planting you will need to keep a careful eye on controlling their growth so they don't completely eclipse their planting partners. As the plants mature, thin and prune out some of the lower dahlia foliage to help keep things in balance. If your dahlias need supporting, try ornamental rusted supports, twisted hazel, willow branches, or birch twigs, all of which add to the overall picture. Alternatively, use thick canes that are well hidden by plants and foliage, and cut them slightly shorter than the plants so they don't stick out of the top like random knitting needles.

Keep on top of dead-heading, water and feed often, and regularly check the moisture level of the surface compost. The underplanting will be much more shallow-rooted than the dahlias, so you might want to use a decorative mulch to prevent it from drying out in hot or windy weather.

Cutting Garden

If you're very lucky and have a garden that's big enough to designate a separate area to grow flowers just for cutting, or have time to tend an allotment, then it's simply rude not to plant at least one decent row of dahlias. Growing them in a straight row or in a grid formation means you can simplify the whole staking operation and have a permanent set of posts and canes in place to support long stems and bigger blooms.

I shared an allotment with a friend a few years ago, mainly because my dahlia passion was outgrowing my garden at home. We collected grass cuttings, cut nettles, and comfrey leaves to spread around the base of plants, and used big blue plastic drums to collect rainwater to feed their thirsty roots. It was lovely when I had the time, and it

A Black-and-White Container Dahlia Display

I GROW MOST of my white dahlias in a series of large pots around my front door. I love to try out lots of different types of plants that contrast strongly and help to show them off. On the list of potential collaborators, no group of plants is ever ruled out—I use grasses, sedges, wild flowers, herbaceous perennials, bulbs, and bedding plants.

I start with two or three plants of six contrasting white dahlia varieties: 'Twyning's After Eight', a jet black dahlia with small, simple, minty white flowers; 'Platinum Blonde', a gorgeous creamy anemone; 'Tsuki Yorine Shisha', a fimbriated ivory cactus; 'Topmix White', a tiny, ultra white lilliput dahlia with daisy-like upward-facing blooms; 'Happy Single Princess', a dark-leaved single with big, veiny flowers; and 'White Star', a great creamy cactus variety.

Some individuals are selected to grow on their own in a pot, and I put others together in contrasting groups of three for my bigger containers. (If you stick to an odd number with any planting scheme, whether in containers or in the ground, you really can't go wrong.)

To these selections of dahlias I add lots of wild carrot plants for extra height. To contrast with the foliage and flower form of the dahlias I use a strappy-leaved variegated sedge called *Carex morrowii* 'Ice Dance' and young lady's mantle plants. Sometimes I add floriferous bedding plants to flow and flower among the understory, like white cultivars of violas and pansies, impatiens, petunias, or wishbone flowers, and sometimes *Bacopa* 'Snowflake' and *Nicotiana langsdorfii* or *N.* 'Cuba Deep Lime'. I also occasionally plant a few *Lilium regale* 'Album' bulbs to trumpet the arrival of dahlia-blooming season. More recently I've been planting a pretty ornamental variety of wild clover called *Trifolium repens* 'Dragon's Blood'. It fills the gaps between the various plants and trails over the edge of the pot. Overall, this quirky planting combination works nicely and blooms well into the autumn.

Growing dahlias on an allotment can be lots of fun. If you add lots of well-rotted horse manure to the soil and mulch the plants heavily, you'll save them from drying out in hot summers.

A rich red, bronze, and burgundy bedding dahlia display featuring *Dahlia* 'Happy Single Flame'.

Bedding dahlias putting on a show in a small urban park visited by hundreds of visitors and city centre residents each day in the heart of Birmingham, England's second-biggest city.

gave me the opportunity to grow some of the big-blooming leafy exhibition varieties that don't always work so well in an herbaceous border but produce the most magnificent and impressive blooms.

In hindsight, maybe I have always been a dahlia-exhibition grower just waiting to blossom. Sadly, I didn't have the time or dedication to devote to them years ago, and I have even less time now. However, the opportunity made me realize just how wonderful it is to grow these huge, brilliant, blowsy exhibition types. It also gave me a certain admiration for a perfectly formed flower.

On the allotment or in the cutting garden, it is perfectly fine to produce prodigious amounts of foliage to fuel the creation of all those incredible blooms. However, for me the volume and appearance of all that dull green foliage of some of the exhibition cultivars distinguishes between a variety perfect for the garden and one just for the cutting garden.

In the garden, all aspects of a dahlia variety must add something to the display. I allow an exception only when the flower is so phenomenal that other aspects of the plant seem peripheral. If your herbaceous borders are very deep and you need some height and drama toward the back, some of the bigger-blooming exhibition or cutting varieties can work brilliantly. You will need access to tweak stakes and supports throughout the season, though. Plenty of interesting foliage plants in front will also help to hide too much mediocre green. Other than that, a cutting patch, an allotment, or a vegetable garden is a good place to grow the taller, leafier types.

Dahlia Walls

LIVING ON THE end of a row of small terraced houses means I have a lot of red brick wall with which to play. I have started to indulge in vertical dahlia experiments with planting pockets. I originally had the idea to have some dahlia graffiti art sprayed outside my back door on a rather uninspiring section of wall. But now I can have the real deal.

My dahlia-wall adventures are just beginning. So far I've kept it simple with my favourite mini double bedding dahlias, grown from seed and tightly planted together. They have flowered all summer long. Next year I'm going to be more adventurous and plant dark-leaved dwarf bedding dahlias, lime- and purple-leaved ornamental sweet potato plants, and magenta, red, and cherry pink trailing bedding verbena. Now I have a new dahlia canvas to re-design and enjoy every year.

Bedding Plants

Some people are quite snobby about bedding dahlias. These are often short, very compact plants that are usually grown from seed. I love them. These hard-working plants are placed in flower beds for just a few months in the summer, and expected to fend for themselves and flower their socks off before the first frost kicks in. Then they are unceremoniously pulled out and assigned to the compost heap, and replaced with spring bulbs and usually winter-flowering pansies. In design terms, blanket bedding displays, where just one type of plant in a single variety is used almost like a floral carpet, can be quite dull and unimaginative. However, when a dahlia bedding mixture is put together with a range of floriferous summer-flowering annuals—such as rudbeckias, verbenas, fiery celosias, and coleus—the display becomes a lot more dynamic. Aesthetically, it's hard to compare these short-lived instant bedding displays to carefully planned out borders containing a range of herbaceous perennials and grasses wafting around among drifts of dahlias, but in terms of bang (or, rather, bloom) for your buck, it's hard to knock them.

You can have lots of flowers for very little effort and cost, and the range of available seed varieties is finally increasing with the appearance of some fun new mixtures and selections. You can find a sea of bright red and orange seed-grown dwarf bedding dahlias providing an impressive splash of colour in Birmingham city centre, England, for example. Bedding dahlias can give any display of pelargoniums, begonias, or impatiens a run for their money. I like to see the dwarf dark-leaved varieties used in displays. There are seed mixtures of these, but often it can be as quick and inexpensive to choose a particularly good variety, bring a few tubers into growth really early under glass, and propagate copious cuttings.

There is an important extra benefit to growing open-centred bedding dahlias. The next time you have the opportunity to observe traditional bedding on a sunny summer day, take a closer look. Count the number of bees, butterflies, hoverflies—pollinators of any kind—across the different types of plants on display. Then compare the insect activity across a bed of dwarf single-bedding dahlias. In my experience, the nectar and pollen resource provided by open-centred dahlias wins every time. It is something I've become more and more aware of in recent years, as the populations of many of our pollinators have declined. We can do a lot to help pollinating insects when we choose what to plant in our containers and window boxes, on our balconies, and in our borders. Planting more open-centred bedding dahlias would be a great start. But it's not only about the environmental advantages. Displays of bedding dahlias are unashamedly colourful. They can help to put a smile on our faces even on the dreariest day.

Dahlias for Borders

- ‘Ann Breckenfelder’
- ‘Arabian Night’
- ‘Black Satin’
- ‘Clair de Lune’
- ‘Comet’
- ‘David Howard’
- ‘Fascination’
- ‘Grenadier’
- ‘Hillcrest Royal’
- ‘Inglebrook Jill’
- ‘Rip City’
- ‘Tahoma Moonshot’

Dark-Leaved Dahlias

- ‘Bee Happy’
- ‘Bishop of Llandaff’
- ‘Candy Eyes’
- ‘Ellen Huston’
- ‘Englehardt’s Matador’
- ‘Knockout’
- ‘Magenta Star’
- ‘Roxy’
- ‘Scura’
- ‘Tally Ho’
- ‘Twyning’s After Eight’
- ‘Twyning’s Revel’

Dahlias for Cut Flowers

- ‘Ambition’
- ‘Bishop of Auckland’
- ‘Crazy Legs’
- ‘Downham Royal’
- ‘Hillcrest Royal’
- ‘Hootenanny’
- ‘Ivanetti’
- ‘Karma Fuchsiana’
- ‘Nuit d’Eté’
- ‘Pearl of Heemstede’
- ‘Sam Hopkins’
- ‘White Star’

Dahlias for Containers

- ‘Bishop of Canterbury’
- ‘Bonne Espérance’
- ‘Collerette Dandy’
- ‘Gallery Art Nouveau’
- ‘Happy Single Flame’
- ‘Keith’s Pet’
- ‘Knockout’
- ‘My-nute Blend’
- ‘Pink Giraffe’
- ‘Rojo Paramo’
- ‘Roxy’

Dahlias for Bees

- ‘Ann Breckenfelder’
- ‘Dannevirke’
- ‘Dovegrove’
- ‘Happy Single Flame’
- ‘Hillcrest Regal’
- ‘Honka Red’
- ‘Magenta Star’
- ‘Moonfire’
- ‘Northwest Cosmos’
- ‘Pooh’
- ‘Teesbrooke Redeye’
- ‘Twyning’s Pink Fish’

Dahlias That Need Little to No Staking

- ‘Bishop of Llandaff’
- ‘Copper Queen’
- ‘David Howard’
- ‘Floorinoor’
- ‘Happy Single Romeo’
- ‘Heartthrob’
- ‘Hootenanny’
- ‘Knockout’
- ‘Moonfire’
- ‘Perfect Partner’
- ‘Totally Tangerine’
- ‘Twyning’s After Eight’

Late-Season Dahlias

- ‘Blue Beard’
- *Dahlia imperialis*
- ‘Englehardt’s Matador’
- ‘Happy Halloween’
- ‘Jeanne D’Arc’
- ‘Junkyard Dog’
- ‘Lavender Chiffon’
- ‘Mambo’
- ‘Nenekazi’
- ‘Sterling Silver’
- ‘Tsuki Yorine Shisha’

Dahlia 'Chimborazo' shines in front of golden variegated pampas grass, as well as surrounded by masses of dancing golden oats.

Planting Pals

My dahlia planting pals are groups of favourite plants or specific varieties that I use when I put together a dahlia border display, but they could just as easily be used with dahlias in container designs. However, this is by no means a definitive list. I am regularly inspired by the planting combinations at the flower shows, gardens, and nurseries that I visit. Grasses, perennials and biennials, tender plants, and annuals all look great with dahlias.

GRASSES

Almost too many grasses to mention look amazing when planted with dahlias. The more species and varieties of grasses I grow, the more I love them. They are my ultimate planting partners for dahlias. These plants are such opposites that you can create an incredibly elegant planting design by limiting the plan to just these two.

When picking grasses, I go for tall and elegant species or varieties, such as *Arundo donax*, calamagrostis, molinia, miscanthus, panicum, pennisetum, and stipa, and combine these with dramatic, deep-coloured dahlias with good foliage. Then I use frothy fellows in confident drifts, like *Anemanthele lessoniana* (syn. *Stipa arundinacea*); *Briza media* 'Limouzi', 'Golden Bee', or 'Russells'; *Chasmanthium latifolium* 'Golden Spangles'; *Deschampsia* 'Pixie Fountain'; and *Hordeum jubatum* or *Milium* 'Yaffle' to add lots of texture and movement at an understory level.

PERENNIALS AND BIENNIALS

Many herbaceous perennials and biennials will grow well with dahlias, but certain genera offer rich pickings of perfect partners. The plants listed here either naturally flower during dahlia season or can be cut back in the spring to flower with the dahlias.

When planting with dahlias, it's good to keep a few things in mind. Depending on which dahlia cultivars you opt for, you may want your plant companions to perform a number of key functions, like screen dull dahlia foliage, contrast strongly in terms of inflorescence shape and form, complement the vibrant colours, and add texture and perhaps a willowy see-through effect. Choose strong, robust, clump-forming perennials and biennials. Fussy herbaceous plants that are a little delicate and can't really fight their own corner often won't thrive next to hungry dahlias.

Acanthus **'Hollard's Gold', 'Summer Beauty',** and ***A. spinosissimus.*** Acanthus are such brilliant garden plants. They are tough and have wonderful leaves and incredible flower spikes. 'Hollard's Gold' has the most gorgeous glossy lime green leaves, and *A. spinosissimus* has deeply divided spiky foliage. These large plants can help hide the rather mediocre foliage of some big garden dahlias. They look great among dark-leaved dahlia varieties too.

Aconitum **'Barkers Variety'.** Monkshood is an impressive plant with tall racemes of large, deep violet-blue flowers. It is perfect among big dahlia varieties in the border. Like dahlias, don't allow it to dry out between waterings. Its foliage can be irritating, so wear gloves when working near it in the border. Note that all parts of this plant are poisonous.

Actaea simplex **'Pink Spike'** is a brilliant, tall, herbaceous perennial that contrasts well in structure and form and carries the flowering well into late autumn.

Agapanthus **'Navy Blue'.** True blue can be a bit of a rarity in the garden at dahlia blooming time, so agapanthus are very welcome. There are all sorts of rich blue varieties to choose from, but this one is my favourite.

Agastache **'Black Adder'.** What a superb plant: a clump-forming deciduous perennial with lilac flowers opening from dark purple buds from midsummer to midautumn. It works well among tall dahlia varieties, as it also loves sun and very well-drained sites. Agastache is fantastic for attracting pollinators into your garden. Cut back right after flowering to encourage a second flush.

Ageratina altissima **'Chocolate'.** This plant has brilliant bronzy-chocolate foliage, is really easy to grow, and works well with grasses. It also sports pretty white flowers, but I grow it primarily for its wonderful foliage.

Alchemilla mollis. I can't recommend this plant enough. It adds brilliant foliage to containers and the front of herbaceous borders, and it's worth growing for cutting too. I use it in lots of quick, unfussy dahlia arrangements. It pops up everywhere, so chop it back before it sets seed or you'll be inundated.

Deep and dramatic varieties like *Dahlia* 'Hillcrest Royal' work well with rich, hot pink *Lychnis coronaria*. In this border at Great Dixter, the vibrant hue is repeated in the towering annual knotweed *Persicaria orientalis* dancing in the distance.

Allium sphaerocephalon. I love this ornamental onion, which flowers later than most and looks wonderful popping up between dahlias.

***Alstroemeria* 'Orange Supreme', 'Charm', 'Indian Summer',** and **'Tessa'.** Tall alstroemerias work really well among dark-leaved dahlia varieties and, like dahlias, if they are left in the ground over winter they need the protection of a generous layer of mulch. There are so many great varieties. 'Indian Summer' is a new dark-leaved alstroemeria that's a bit shorter, so it's perfect for container planting with dwarf and container dahlia varieties.

Angelica archangelica, A. gigas, and ***A.* 'Ebony'.** These huge biennial umbels make wonderful spot plants in a mixed dahlia planting. 'Ebony' has wonderful matte black foliage and *A. gigas* has beautiful rich burgundy umbels, but the glossy green *A. archangelica* is pretty impressive too.

***Anthemis* 'Sauce Hollandaise'** and other varieties, such as **'E.C. Buxton'** and **'Gold Mound',** can help to blend and soften strong yellow dahlias in planting schemes. If you cut back anthemis plants to one-third of their height in early to midspring, they will flower later and longer alongside your dahlias. Orange and dark-leaved dahlia varieties and red hot pokers look amazing dotted among these plants.

***Aster* 'Coombe Fishacre', 'Calliope', 'Lye End Beauty', *A. novae-angliae* 'Alma Potschke', *A. lateriflorus* 'Bleke Bet', *A.* ×*frikartii* 'Mönch',** and ***A. amellus* 'King George'** are just a few of my favourite asters to plant with dahlias and carry on the floral fireworks well into the autumn. Choose mildew-resistant rich violet-blues like 'King George', deep pinks, and varieties with dark bronze foliage.

Cephalaria gigantea. The lofty flowers of this primrose-yellow giant scabious are beautiful among tall dahlia varieties.

***Chamaenerion angustifolium* 'Stahl Rose'.** This plant is rampant and a bit of a thug, but the paler pink variety is gorgeous. Keep it in check by digging around it in late spring.

Crambe cordifolia. The very tall branching panicles of tiny flowers contrast well with the comparatively large blooms of dahlia varieties. It is magical.

***Crocosmia* 'Lucifer', 'Emily McKenzie', 'Paul's Best Yellow', 'Zeal Giant',** and **'Rowallane Yellow'.** Crocosmias grow very well with dahlias. They love the same open, sunny locations and rich, free-draining soils. 'Lucifer' is a classic robust variety.

Cynara cardunculus. The silvery acanthus-like leaves of cardoon thistles look great in a border with dark-leaved dahlia varieties. Bees adore their huge tufty flower heads. When the plants mature and produce flower spikes, you can thin out many of the bigger bottom leaves.

Daucus carota. All sorts of umbels work brilliantly among dahlias, as the flat-topped, inverted umbrella-like flower heads are such a contrasting flower form. *Dahlia* 'Happy Single Princess' (see page 44) looks wonderful when planted with wild carrot. Also look out for the devilishly delicious burgundy-and-black *D. carota* 'Black Knight'.

***Delphinium* 'Black Night', 'Finsteraarhorn',** and **'Volkerfrieden'.** Lots of tall delphinium varieties make great planting companions with dahlias, especially the early flowering varieties that can be cut back for a second flush to coincide with peak dahlia-blooming season.

***Echinacea purpurea* 'Magnus', 'Rubinstern', 'Ruby Giant', 'Vintage Wine',** and **'White Swan'.** There are so many great cone flowers to plant with dahlias. I love the rich pink and purples the most; they seem to be the toughest. *Echinacea purpurea* 'Magnus' is my favourite.

Echinops ritro* 'Veitch's Blue', *E. bannaticus* 'Taplow Blue',** and ***E. sphaerocephalus. These blue-and-silver globes of spiky floral fun look wonderful with pretty much everything in a herbaceous border and, like dahlias, they love good, rich soil and open, sunny locations.

Eryngium* 'Sapphire Blue'** and ***E. planum. Even more spiky and silver-blue than echinops, sea hollies work well with medium to small dahlias. Make sure you give them plenty of room, as they love the sun even more than dahlias do. There are so many wonderful varieties, but I prefer these two.

***Eucomis comosa* 'Sparkling Burgundy'.** This spiky, fizzy pineapple lily is the best of the bunch. It's brilliant among short, dark-leaved dahlias.

Euphorbia. So many euphorbias make brilliant planting companions with dahlias. The incredible range of yellows, greens, oranges, and reds in their foliage and flowers throughout the spring and summer months add texture and colour, while in autumn they turn through beautiful fiery shades. *Euphorbia sikkimensis* is a particular favourite.

Ferula communis. Giant fennel has the frothiest blue-green foliage you ever will see, as well as an amazing gigantic flower spike. It's a jaw-dropping spot plant that will tower above even giant decorative dinnerplate dahlias.

Foeniculum vulgare and ***F. vulgare* 'Giant Bronze'.** Plants like fennel, purple *Verbena bonariensis*, and spiky silver-blue *Eryngium planum* can instantly inject texture into a dahlia-planting scheme.

***Geranium psilostemon* 'Patricia', 'Anne Folkard',** and **'Sandrine'.** The larger hardy geranium varieties with big leaves and sprawling habit work well among dahlias. There is a big contrast in terms of leaf and flower form, and I love these intense, brightly coloured cultivars.

***Helenium* 'Moerheim Beauty', 'Rubinzwerg',** and **'Sahin's Early Flowerer'.** There are many hardy, colourful, helenium varieties that look amazing and grow well among dahlias. They are tough, easy-to-manage plants, and they provide months of colour, are attractive to pollinating insects, and seem unaffected by most pests and diseases. I particularly love the deep orange and red cultivars.

***Helianthus salicifolius* 'Bitter Chocolate'.** I grow this perennial sunflower for its amazing foliage, although it does have small flowers in the autumn. It's very tall indeed, and thus one for the back of the border, but it adds so much texture. It's a fabulous plant.

Plants like purple *Verbena bonariensis* add an extra layer of texture to this dahlia display.

Actaea simplex 'Pink Spike' is a useful and contrasting flower that accentuates pink and pale dahlia varieties in a planting scheme.

Helianthus **'Miss Mellish', 'Lemon Queen'.** The big, rich, bright yellow blooms of 'Miss Melish' look wonderful among tall dahlia varieties in deep rich shades. Keep an eye on this plant, though—it's a runner and will want to take over. As it pops up in late spring, dig around it and keep it in check. 'Lemon Queen' is another brilliant perennial sunflower, but a lovely pale yellow colour. This tall one is also a thug and meant for the back of the border.

Hemerocallis **'Frans Hals', 'Golden Zebra',** and **'Stafford'.** This is perhaps more of an opening act than a planting partner. It's good to have some extra floral interest in early summer, however, while young green dahlia plants are building themselves up for their main performance. I find that, apart from a few roses and lilies, there can be a green gap as most of the tulips, peonies, and spring herbaceous fade away. Daylilies span this period well, and they are such easy, no-nonsense perennials to grow. There are hundreds of varieties, but these three are my favourites.

Heuchera **'Magnum'.** Among the many heucheras, heucherellas, and tiarellas out there, this new, big-leaved variety has become an instant hit. Its massive purple leaves span 25 cm (10 in.) across. The leaves are burgundy and boldly lobed, with dark veins and a slight silvery sheen. It enjoys semi-shade, so placing it among medium to tall dahlia varieties should keep it happy.

Knautia **'Melton Pastels'.** These plants, which in my garden are effectively seedlings of *K. macedonica*, are more robust than the parent plant, and I have let them grow across my back garden. I love the tiny pincushion flowers in all their different shades, from almost magenta to the palest pink. With good silver-green foliage, this plant looks gorgeous and contrasts well among rich pink and purple dahlias.

***Kniphofia* 'Tawny King', 'Nancy's Red', 'Mount Etna',** and **'Rich Echoes'.** Red hot pokers make great bedfellows for dahlias, but they need lots of sun to flower well, so give them room and space plants carefully. These look totally wonderful among rich red, orange, purple, and magenta dark-leaved dahlia varieties. 'Tawny King' has dark bronze stems and flowers that start off orange and turn through apricot to cream.

***Lobelia* 'Tania'.** My favourite is this really vivid magenta-flowered lobelia. You can find lots of other good, rich varieties, such as the pink-and-bronze 'Russian Princess', red-and-bronze 'Bee's Flame', or cotton candy–coloured 'Pink Elephant'. They love rich moist soil and good drainage, so they work well with dahlias.

***Lychnis coronaria*.** This plant will seed around happily in borders, and its silvery leaves can help lift the flowers and foliage of neighbouring plants. Deep puce-pink flowers are a fabulous contrast to its overall silveriness.

***Lysimachia atropurpurea* 'Beaujolais'.** Purple gooseneck loosestrife is a biennial or short-lived perennial in my garden. It has strong red-purple flowers with gray-green leaves. It seems to love moist, rich soil, so it grows well with dahlias. It's great for cutting.

***Mathiasella bupleuroides* 'Green Dream'.** Once you see this curious rich lime green umbel, you just have to have it. Since I started growing 'Green Dream', I find that no green-and-white planting scheme is complete without it.

***Monarda*.** Bergamot and bee balm associate well with dahlias. Both are quite tall and hungry, and they love moist, rich soil. The downside is that both can suffer terribly from mildew in damp, wet summers, so choose the more mildew-resistant varieties and use a preventive organic milk spray treatment (see page 217).

***Penstemon* 'Sour Grapes'.** This is a spectacular variety, and any plant that brings to mind *The Banana Splits*, my favourite children's puppet show from the 1970s, has to be a good thing. It has great colour and needs a sunny site and good drainage to flower well.

***Persicaria amplexicaulis* 'Atrosanguinea'.** The spiked inflorescences of plants like persicarias contrast really well with dahlias in a mixed border planting. This is a tough and robust perennial.

***Ratibida pinnata*.** A yellow cone flower that requires good drainage and lots of sun. I adore its long, ribbon-like golden petals. You'll find good silvery foliage on a tall plant, but it's not a thug. This plant moves beautifully in the summer breeze and looks great with *Verbena bonariensis* and the taller dark-leaved dahlia varieties. Give it room to breathe among dahlias or it won't be happy.

***Rudbeckia laciniata* 'Herbstsonne'.** This is a really useful rudbeckia to use with strong yellow, bright orange, deep purple, and rich magenta dahlia varieties. Let all those vibrant shades fight it out. 'Herbstsonne' can get extremely big, leafy, and tall; it's a bit of a brute. Cut it back to the ground in midspring and it will flower later but on slightly shorter, more manageable stems. Lift and divide regularly, or it can take over. *Rudbeckia fulgida* var. *deamii*, a classic, shorter variety, is brilliant. It produces golden daisies with black button noses and runs around nicely among dahlia varieties all over my back garden. I love it.

***Salvia nemerosa* 'Caradonna'** and ***S. verticillata* 'Purple Rain'.** Blue-purple spikes that bees and insect pollinators go mad for. They contrast nicely in their overall shape and flower form with dahlias. There are lots of great salvias to choose from, but these two hardy perennial ones are super.

A rich combination of dark-leaved *Dahlia* 'David Howard' and *Salvia* 'Indigo Spires' at Great Dixter House and Gardens, East Sussex, England.

***Sanguisorba* 'Pink Tanna'.** This is my favourite burnet, as it's upright and has lovely tiny bottle brush–like spikes of pure rosy pink and white, plus good gray-green foliage. Like *Verbena bonariensis*, sanguisorbas or burnets are really useful if you want a gentle transparent effect in a border. *Sanguisorba* 'Pink Elephant', *S. menziesii*, and *S. obtusa* are also good and a bit taller; they are a little floppy and need some support. They have good contrasting form and flower with dahlias and look great among dark-leaved and medium to short border varieties.

***Sedum* 'Purple Emperor', 'Matrona', 'Red Cauli', and 'Karfunkelstein'.** *Sedum spectabile* and *S. telephium* hybrids and cultivars, especially the deep burgundy and maroon ones like 'Purple Emperor', look good with dahlias. Sedums are compact, clump-forming deciduous perennials, and the bees, butterflies, and hoverflies adore them. The taller cultivars can sometimes get a little bit too succulent and fall over in late summer, so cut them back to one-third of their height in mid- to late spring. They will flower later, but they'll be slightly shorter and better able to support their huge, flat flower heads. If you want a knockout shorter one, try 'Karlfunkelstein' or shorter still 'Red Cauli'.

***Thalictrum* 'Black Stockings' and 'Elin'.** These two varieties of meadow rue are somewhat similar to *Verbena bonariensis* in terms of what they offer in texture and form, but are perhaps even more delicious. 'Black Stockings' has gorgeous lavender-purple flowers on jet black stems. It is tall and willowy, with dainty foliage. It needs support, but

A bold drift of white *Cosmos bipinnatus* 'Purity' creates the perfect backdrop and an opportunity for this apricot semi-cactus dahlia to shine and take centre stage.

it is stunning and well worth growing. It couldn't be more of a contrast to a dahlia, and looks great among grasses too.

Veronicastrum virginicum. I love the pink, lilac, and purple forms, such as 'Lavendelturm', 'Fascination', and 'Pink Glow'. This brilliant, tall, herbaceous perennial reaches for the sky with slender, erect stems and wonderfully narrow, serrated leaves arranged in whorls. It has lovely long pointy racemes of tiny flowers.

TENDER PLANTS

If your objective is to inject a tropical or exotic flavour into a dahlia-planting scheme, tender plants are well worth the effort. The following perennials are my favourites, and they can play a fabulous supporting role and add extra lushness and excitement.

Begonia luxurians. An unusual cane-stemmed species with palm-like leaves that give it a real jungle feel. It is pretty robust and upright and it can grow quite tall, so give it room. The amazing oversize leaves are what growing this plant is all about; the deeply divided slender lobes have gorgeous coppery undersides. This exceptional plant is featured in the exotic garden at Great Dixter.

***Canna* 'Durban', 'Erebus', 'Pacific Beauty', 'Pretoria',** and **'Valentine'.** Cannas are got-to-have-it plants for a sub-tropical display because of their fantastic foliage and flowers. The stripy dark burgundy or yellow-green leaves add so much, and many are incredibly floriferous if given plenty of warmth and light, plus some good, rich soil.

***Colocasia esculenta, C.* 'Black Magic'.** This plant has big, dramatic, elephant-ear foliage to die for. 'Black Magic' is incredible—if black leaves are your thing, you won't be disappointed. However, it is a bit of a diva, and not the easiest plant to overwinter in temperate climates (although you can store large rhizomes dry until spring). Once you gently coax it up to speed with bottom heat for a few weeks in mid- to late spring, it quickly gets greedy, so feed it daily with a dilute half-strength solution. It will sulk in cool summers, but will grow like wildfire when given warm weather, plenty of moisture, and rich soil.

Ensete ventricosum. The Abyssinian banana grows at altitude in its native Ethiopia, so it's far more at home in temperate summer weather than you might expect, but it's not completely hardy. This plant can become a beast if you're fortunate enough to have somewhere to keep it frost free in the winter. Ultimately it can grow up to 12 m (40 ft.) in the wild, but in temperate gardens I've never seen one more than about 3 m (10 ft.) tall. It has fantastic paddle-shaped leaves with a burgundy midrib.

Eupatorium capillifolium. Sometimes called dog fennel, this is an unusual foliage plant that I first encountered in the exotic garden at Great Dixter. Totally unlike other *Eupatorium* species, it has tall feathery stems covered in fine, bright green, hair-like foliage. It has a gentle see-through quality, and brings heaps of fine filigree texture to the table.

Musa basjoo. In milder temperatures, the Japanese banana is often grown permanently outside in sheltered gardens, although the tall main stems require a substantial amount of protection from frosts. Large, bright green leaves arching up from a thick main stem bring an instant tropical atmosphere to any planting.

Salvia. So many of the late, summer-flowering, tender salvias bring an exotic hummingbird flutter to a jungle-like planting scheme. The delicate flighty blooms contrast beautifully with deep, dark dahlia varieties. I love big pink *S. involucrata*, but so many

Ravishing red *Dahlia* 'Witteman's Superba' revels among a plethora of shrubs, grasses, and herbaceous perennials at Great Dixter.

other varieties are equally sumptuous. *Salvia buchananii*, *S. curviflora*, and *S.* 'Wendy's Wish' are all strong, rich, delicious pinks that I can't resist. On par with agapanthus, salvias also win a late-summer blue ribbon. If blue is your colour, try *S. cacaliifolia*, *S. guaranitica* 'Blue Enigma', *S. patens* 'Cambridge Blue' and 'Guanajuato', or *S.* 'Indigo Spires'.

***Solenostemon* (syn. *Coleus*) 'Chocolate Mint', 'Black Dragon',** and **'Wizard Velvet Red'.** These are just three of the many vividly variegated and dark-leaved coleus to try. The plant is easy to grow from seed each year.

Tetrapanax papyrifer. A deciduous shrub with massive, fabulously felty leaves. If grown in good, rich soil and given lots of feed, it can put on lots of leaves up to 80 cm (32 in.) across.

Verbena bonariensis. This is a short-lived perennial best grown as a hardy annual. I think the strongest plants come from heel cuttings of non-flowering shoots taken in late summer and overwintered. I never tire of it. It will sow itself around in sheltered gardens and come through mild winters unscathed. It is possibly the ultimate planting companion for dahlias. They are such opposites, but made for each other.

ANNUALS

Hardy and half-hardy annuals bring even more texture and excitement to the dahlia table, making for a very richly planted border. The following are those I just couldn't live without.

Atriplex hortensis* var. *rubra. Many dahlia varieties have quite unexciting green foliage, so creating texture in planting combinations is important. One of my favourite combinations is to plant fennel, both green and bronze varieties, with red orache, *A. hortensis* var. *rubra*, and black- or purple-leaved shrubs such as *Sambucus* 'Black Lace'.

Cleome hassleriana. Spider flowers in white, pinks, and purples look brilliant with dahlias. A bit like *Verbena bonariensis*, they are tall and elegant, and move gently in the wind. They contrast well in terms of flower form, and they bloom well into autumn.

Cosmos bipinnatus. This is my number-one go-to half-hardy annual. I use it to splash even more colour around in a mixed dahlia border. I love all the varieties, but the deep pinks like 'Dazzler', 'Rubenza', and 'Antiquity' are my absolute favourites, followed closely by the tall white 'Purity'.

Leonotis leonurus. Lion's tail, or wild dagga, hails from southern and South Africa. It's a very architectural plant with vertical spires with globe-like clusters of bright tangerine flowers along its length—it reminds me of the tall, elegant minarets in Marrakesh. This half-hardy perennial is best grown as an annual in cool, temperate regions. Like verbena, it is the perfect plant to grow among dahlias. Sow it as early as you can to get the biggest plants and the longest flowering period.

Nicotiana langsdorfii and ***N. mutabilis.*** I love these two charming, half-hardy annual tobacco flowers. They work well planted in front of tall dahlias, as their masses of little blooms provide lots of floral interest and spice up the dull green foliage. Planted among slightly shorter, dark-leaved dahlias, their bobbing fairy-hat flowers dance about in the breeze.

Persicaria orientalis. This giant annual knotweed is quite something. It self-seeds when grown in warmer regions, and it has bright pink floral tassels. It's a terrific and unusual plant, and quite a talking point in late summer when it's flowering at full throttle and dangling above your tallest dahlias.

***Ricinus communis* 'Carmencita'.** The red castor oil plant is really a tall, well-branched evergreen shrub, but often grown as an annual in sub-tropical–style plantings with dahlias. It has glorious big-lobed, dark bronze-red leaves, red stems, and dark red porcupine capsules covered in soft spines in late summer and autumn.

Rudbeckia hirta. Rudbeckias are at their absolute best in late summer and early autumn. I love the large jolly flowers of lots of *R. hirta* varieties, but particularly the taller single ones. My current favourites are 'Marmalade', 'Autumn Colours', and 'Cherry Brandy'. They reflect the changing colours of the season to come. They are inexpensive and very easy to grow from seed, and very much at home among dahlias in full sun on rich soils.

***Tithonia rotundifolia* 'Torch'.** The Mexican sunflower is an annual that's pretty quick and easy to grow each year from seed. 'Torch' has bright orange daisy-like blooms from midsummer until late autumn. Its dark green lobed foliage is also attractive. In no time at all plants will grow up 2 m (6 ft.). If you love orange as much as I do, you have to grow this plant among your dahlias. Put it in front of dark green or black foliage to really show it off.

Zinnia. Along with annual rudbeckias, zinnias can help to really up the floral ante at the lower levels in a tall dahlia display. I love the taller varieties of *Z. elegans*. The Magellan series performs well and is available in some great vivid colours ('Cherry', 'Scarlet', and 'Pink' are my favourites). I've also discovered the Zahara series of shorter, much bushier plants of *Z. marylandica*. 'Fire', 'Double Cherry', and 'Coral Rose' are all marvellous.

UNDERSTANDING DAHLIAS

Dahlia 'Happy Tip Red', a compact plant with dark foliage, is ideal for containers and small gardens.

Dahlias originate in Central and South America. There are approximately 36 species. The majority of wild populations of species dahlias can be found in specific regions of Mexico, but some species grow as far south as Guatemala, and there are reports of others naturalized in the foothills of Peru. The plants that European explorers discovered in the 1500s did not look as complex or impressive as the highly bred varieties we are now familiar with, although I imagine even the species plants caused quite a stir. Double dahlias did exist, however. Drawings from this time prove that the Aztecs grew double-flowered hybrids. Most of the wild species have quite simple, single, open-centred blooms with just one or two rows of outer florets that have larger, showy petals.

In the early days of dahlia cultivation in Europe, French horticulturalists experimented with growing them as a food crop. These trials, at the Jardin des Plantes in Paris, did not last long, as the tubers were very bitter. Recently, with a resurgence of interest in growing new and unusual food crops, I have noticed dahlias being marketed as "dahlia yams." Unlike potatoes, which are stem tubers and store starch, dahlias are root tubers and store inulin, a type of fiber. I am amazed that anyone would recommend them for eating. At best they are bland and need their taste masked with something more palatable.

Unlike the delightful waxy or flowery texture of potatoes, dahlias can be gritty and, a bit like Jerusalem artichokes, can leave you feeling bloated and gassy. I think those French gardeners knew best. Let's be glad we have the potato and leave well enough alone.

It didn't take long for dahlias to become the darling of nursery owners and estate gardeners in Europe. By the 1800s, this exciting new plant was being exploited and enjoyed. All sorts of new colours and forms were about to be bred. New varieties were derived from deliberate crosses and chance seedlings, and the first truly fully double dahlias were arriving on the gardening scene.

The Victorian and Edwardian eras were the heyday of the dahlia. By the time the young Queen Victoria took the throne, a South American Cinderella was becoming the new monarch of the gardening world. In the 1840s, dahlia plants were setting the horticultural world alight both in the United Kingdom and the United States, and in 1851 the Great Exhibition in London brought the dahlia to people of all social classes, cultures, and countries. Thus began Dahlia mania, an obsession with the plants that is said to be of a similar magnitude to the tulip craze of the 1600s. The demand for new types was intense, and thus began a race between head gardeners and nursery owners to breed new colours and forms. Dahlias had become status symbols, and the number and range of forms and colours were often seen as a big floral show of wealth.

In Britain the dahlia soon became an exhibition flower that could be grown to the most perfect and exacting standards, and in 1881 the National Dahlia Society was founded. This trend for exhibiting dahlias spread to other countries in the British Empire, and in the early 1900s dahlia societies and exhibitions were growing popular in the United States and New Zealand.

The Plant

Dahlias are a type of daisy. They belong to one of the biggest plant families in the floral kingdom: Asteraceae, formerly referred to as Compositae, the daisy or sunflower family. They are cousins of asters, chrysanthemums, rudbeckias, gerberas, marigolds, marguerites, cone flowers, and the little daisies in your lawn, to name but a few. This family contains the most colourful, carefree, and blissful blooms imaginable.

As with other members of Asteraceae, dahlias can appear to be just one bloom or flower, but in fact they are a mass of tiny individual flowers, called an *inflorescence*. There are many different types of inflorescence, and in dahlias it is quite specialized and often referred to as a *capitulum*. A capitulum is composed of numerous individual flowers that sit directly on top of a structure known as a *receptacle*. These tiny sessile flowers are called *florets*.

There are two types of florets, disc and ray. The centre of the capitulum is composed of unfussy florets that resemble tiny tubes. These are the disc florets. The outer, showier part of the capitulum comprises florets with a single ligulate, which is a strap-like petal. These are the ray florets, essentially the petals of a dahlia flower. Many other forms of dahlias are complete exhibitionists with an inflorescence that is made up of all kinds of extravagant ray florets. They truly are an explosion of floral fun. Overall, the inflorescence

A butterfly feeding from a disc floret of a collerette dahlia. The tiny florets around the edge of the disc are the first to mature. Over a number of days, in a spiral formation, the rest of the tight disc florets will open. The floret right at the centre of the bloom is the last to mature.

or capitulum still appears to resemble a single bloom. This phenomenon is quite widespread among flowering plants, and is often referred to as *pseudanthia*.

It is difficult to quote exact heights and spreads of dahlia varieties, as there are so many factors at play. A young plant started from a cutting and flowering for the first time won't be the same size as a mature one that has been grown from a large tuber that has been successfully overwintered and mulched with a thick layer of manure and, as a result, is blooming like a floral rocket in overdrive. Almost identical plants grown in different geographical locations under very similar growing conditions can vary hugely in their maximum height and spread, and as with all garden plants, the type of soil they are growing in can be a big influence too.

Dahlias respond to lots of water and nutrients, which play a huge part in their overall size, as does the amount and quality of sunlight each plant receives. I'm often astonished at how tall, lush, and substantial dahlia plants are in the fields of professional breeders and growers. However, these plants are usually perfectly irrigated and fertilized, and exposed to lots of bright, open, sunny weather. I'm perfectly happy with my own specimens of the same variety at home, even though they are often slightly smaller in stature. But I grow the majority of my dahlias among many other types of plants, and in my densely planted garden, there is competition for water, nutrients, and sunlight. The height and spread for the plants described in this book are an approximation of the size of a two-year-old plant grown in good garden conditions.

Flower Forms

The many dahlia societies across the world have officially divided dahlia flower forms into different groups or classes: anemone, collerette, ball, pompon, and cactus. The names can seem a little daunting for the uninitiated, but these terms are actually simple and helpful, as they describe the shape or appearance of the individual flowers. You can very quickly become adept at recognizing the group or class to which a dahlia belongs.

Many of the groups are then further divided by the overall size of the bloom. So, for example, a cactus dahlia could be a giant cactus, a large cactus, or a medium, small, or even miniature cactus. Before you know it, you'll develop an eye for spotting the different sorts and sizes and will become a bona fide dahlia-spotter. You'll be able to impress all your friends with your ability to determine a waterlily from a cactus, and a medium decorative from a pompon.

After growing dahlias for nearly 15 years, I'm not entirely exactly sure of the boundaries between a giant and a large, or a medium and small. I often just go on instinct. Even if you're not growing to exhibition standards, these extra sub-divisions of bloom size are useful when choosing new varieties for the garden from catalogues or on websites, as they offer a rough idea of the size of the blooms. However, I recommend visiting growers and nurseries at the height of the flowering season so you can see a variety of plants at their best, and compare the sizes of blooms.

Petal forms and their arrangement largely determine the different groups of dahlias. Decorative and waterlily dahlias have flat, broad petals. Cactus and semi-cactus types have rolled, pointed, almost quill-like petals. Ball and pompon types have globular flowers with formal, orderly, rolled petals. These are the main, well-known groups, but there are exciting new developments all the time. A huge variety of forms has always existed, but there has been an explosion in the number of new varieties across a wide range of types. Some fantastic new flower forms are appearing, and others have been re-discovered. Some of these dahlias were previously grouped under the term *miscellaneous*. Now we have peony and double orchid types, chrysanthemum types, stars, stellars, singles, semi-doubles, multi-layered collerettes, carnation types, spoon-petalled types, and petite types.

The following groups of dahlias are types that I simply love to grow. I've loosely based the descriptions on the official groups recognized by either the American Dahlia Society or the National Dahlia Society in the United Kingdom.

SINGLE DAHLIAS

Single dahlias have blooms with just one outer ring of florets with showy ligulate petals around a central disc of tiny florets. This inner disc of tight florets transforms as the flower develops, and bright yellow or orange pollen suddenly appears on stamens in concentric rings, often vividly contrasting with the colour of the tiny petals. All sorts of pollinators home in on these hotspots. Single dahlias are becoming popular with gardeners who want to provide something special for insects that are still active in late summer and autumn.

In the past, gardeners rather over-looked the potential of single varieties, and mainly planted short single varieties (often known as dwarf bedding types) closely together in traditional bedding displays. Now singles are one of the most exciting groups of dahlias to grow. So many new varieties being bred are perfect for small-garden situations and container displays. Some are highly valued for their attractive, dark-coloured leaves, while others have glossy, frothy, or deeply cut foliage. This ever-increasing range of single varieties with contrasting floral and foliage characteristics is stoking the fires of the dahlia revolution.

Dahlia 'Happy Single Princess', Single

STAR OR SINGLE ORCHID DAHLIAS

Star or single orchid dahlias are a type of single dahlia. They have a distinct central disc of tiny florets and just one outer ring of ray florets with more showy petals. These outer petals distinguish the group. They are rather elongated, and often curled inward at some point along their length, which gives the bloom the appearance of a mini floral wind turbine. These varieties look great planted in confident drifts that display a mass of distinctive propeller-petal blooms. My favourites include the Honka range of cultivars, particularly 'Honka Rose' and 'Honka Surprise', as well as a variety called 'Midnight Star'.

Some single orchid varieties, such as 'Juuls Allstar', are also pleasantly scented. If you've ever imagined a gentle, sweet-smelling floral version of a child's plastic seaside windmill, this dahlia variety is just that.

Dahlia 'Classic Rosamunde', Peony

Dahlia 'Twyning's Candy', Single

Dahlia 'Bishop of Llandaff', Peony

Dahlia 'Honka Surprise', Star

Dahlia 'Honey', Anemone

Dahlia 'Lemon Puff', Anemone

PEONY DAHLIAS

A good example of a peony dahlia is 'Bishop of Llandaff', one of the most popular dark-leaved dahlias. Peony dahlias are similar to the singles, but this group usually has more than one ring of outer showy florets with quite large voluptuous petals—often two, three, or four rows of them. A few of the petals close to the central disc are often quite small and slightly curled or twisted, lending a slightly tousled appearance to the overall bloom.

ANEMONE DAHLIAS

There is something bizarre, yet enthralling, about anemone dahlias. The blooms consist of an outer ring of relatively normal ray florets with flat showy petals. But in the centre, masses of tiny elongated flowers erupt to form a sort of crazy floral pincushion. It's a quirky dome of tubular florets all crammed tightly together, causing the bloom to almost morph into a powder puff. These dahlias often come in some very eccentric colour combinations, and some varieties should probably live on *Sesame Street* and sing songs with Big Bird, Elmo, Bert, and Ernie. But I have to admit, I rather adore them. A flower that can make me smile, and sometimes even laugh out loud, is very welcome in my garden. I am in danger of developing a strange addiction to them. They may have the same effect on you.

COLLERETTE DAHLIAS

In many ways, collerettes—originally developed in France centuries ago—are a fancy type of single dahlia that has been beautifully developed and perfected by lots of great breeding work. Like single types, the bloom usually has one outer ring of standard flat ray petals and a clear open centre made up of lots and lots of tiny flowers. Its distinguishing

Dahlia 'Wowie', Collerette

Dahlia 'Jane Horton', Collerette

feature is the dainty collar of tiny florets surrounding the disc in the centre. (There is clear access to these tiny tubular flowers, so collerettes are a solid favourite among all sorts of pollinators.) In many popular varieties, this flirty ring of petaloids is a contrasting colour to the vibrant outer petals and adds an exotic feel to the look of the bloom. In addition to these contrasting-colour types, some wonderful collerettes come in delicate pastel shades, while in others the collar florets are just a slight tint, shade, or tone different in colour.

CACTUS AND SEMI-CACTUS DAHLIAS

'Banker', a bright orange, verging on red, cactus dahlia was the first dahlia variety I ever grew. It's a glorious explosion of pointy, bright tangerine petals that left me quite dazzled. The first cactus dahlias, cultivated in the Netherlands in the late 1800s, were named *Les Etoiles de Diable*, which means stars of the devil. I imagine their red-hot pronged petals probably invited the appellation.

Cactus and semi-cactus dahlias are really two separate groups, but I find them very hard to tell apart. All are fully double, which means that every individual tiny floret that makes up the bloom has a long, pointy petal that is rolled inward along its length. This gives the appearance of a ball of spiky quills, almost like a floral porcupine. The blooms come in all sorts of sizes, as the length of each individual pointy petal affects the overall size of the bloom.

The intriguing pointy petals of cactus and semi-cactus blooms can be quite straight or curved inward toward the tip or even twisted slightly along the length of the petal. When they are twisted, the resulting bloom has a fabulously shaggy appearance.

In the semi-cactus types, the petals of the individual flowers that make up the bloom

Dahlia 'Rawhide', Waterlily

Dahlia 'Karma Choc', Waterlily

Dahlia 'Marlene Joy'. Close-up photography of these dahlias is otherworldly. If you like cactus types, you'll totally adore these. 'Marlene Joy' is the first fimbriated semi-cactus dahlia variety I grew, and it's still one of my favourites.

Dahlia 'Fuzzy Wuzzy' has one or two small splits or snips at the tip of the petals, which lends a sawtoothed or zigzag effect. These blooms look like they have been snipped with pinking shears. The overall effect can be reminiscent of carnation petals.

Dahlia 'Banker', Cactus

Dahlia 'Hillcrest Royal', Cactus

are broader and flatter at the base and taper and roll toward the tip. Overall, its appearance is a little less spiky and almost softer in the centre of the bloom.

As a general rule, the more spidery the dahlia bloom is, or the more it resembles a spiny urchin-like creature living on the ocean floor, the more likely it's a true cactus. All good dahlia displays need a few spiky cactus varieties to liven things up a bit. 'Hillcrest Royal' is one of my all-time top choices. It's an absolutely first-class cactus cultivar.

FIMBRIATED OR LACINIATED DAHLIAS

If spiky is your thing—and it's definitely mine—these dahlias will hook you in. Their petals are further divided at the tip, and each one is split like a tiny fishtail or the forked tongue of a snake. When I first encountered one I was completely drawn in by the twists and flicks of the petals around the fringe of the bloom.

A split in the tips of petals can be observed in a number of dahlia forms, not just cactus and semi-cactus types. During a recent visit to dahlia gardens in Japan, I was intrigued by the popularity of fimbriated giant decorative dahlia varieties.

WATERLILY DAHLIAS

Waterlilies are another fully double group of dahlias, but the florets have very broad, flat petals that are often rolled inward very slightly at the edges. The overall appearance of the bloom feels very delicate and is similar to a true waterlily flower. If you want to have some fun, these broad shallow blooms float beautifully on water, and I have cut them and put them among the leaves of waterlily plants in a barrel pond, which fooled many of my non-gardening friends. This group of dahlias makes brilliant cut flowers, as the stems of many varieties have been bred to be very straight and long. *Dahlia* 'Karma Choc' is totally gorgeous.

Dahlia 'Pink Giraffe', Double orchid

Dahlia 'Tiny Treasure', Pompom

DOUBLE ORCHID DAHLIAS

Double orchid dahlias have fully double blooms with many rows of ray florets and at first show no disc. As the bloom matures, a small central, almost triangular, group of disc florets is often revealed. The numerous rows of ray florets are narrowly lance shaped and also roll inward slightly. There are relatively few double orchid varieties, and they are similar to peony, star, and stellar types. You can find them under the "miscellaneous" category on some websites. My favourite double orchid dahlia is 'Pink Giraffe'. It's a bizarre striped-pink swizzle stick, and quite an old variety.

BALL AND POMPON DAHLIAS

It has taken me a little longer to appreciate these rather formal, fully double, globular wonders of the dahlia world. However, I'm convinced that it's only so long before they completely draw you in. Up close these blooms and their expanding rows of petals are something of a mathematician's dream. Anyone familiar with the Fibonacci series of numbers—where each number is the sum of the previous two numbers—will marvel at the petal arrangement of these blooms, from the centre of the flower to the outer edge. They offer up an infinite spherical swirl of florets, with fold upon fold of perfect petals.

Pompons are really just a heightened mini form of a ball dahlia, but even more globular and lollipop-like. The petals of both balls and pompons are blunt or slightly rounded at the tip. Small pompons are, without a doubt, the cutest dahlias. They were named after the bobbles on the jolly hats of French sailors. Balls and pompons are lots of fun, and if you love growing your own cut flowers, these dahlias definitely add a different dimension to an arrangement. There is something slightly vintage and cool about them. You can make the most wonderfully retro dolly mixture dahlia display with them.

Dahlia 'Giraffe', Double orchid

Dahlia 'Sylvia', Ball

Informal decorative *Dahlia* 'Gilt Edge' has wavy, more relaxed petals than a formal variety.

Dahlia 'Sweet Content', with neat, uniform, precisely arranged petals, is a good example of a formal decorative.

Dahlia 'Hugs and Kisses', Stellar

Dahlia 'Verrone's Taylor Swift', Stellar

DECORATIVE DAHLIAS

Decorative is a bit of an umbrella term when it comes to dahlias. Essentially it covers a huge group, ranging from the truly humongous dinnerplate dahlias with massive heads of petals to average-size flowers. Decorative dahlias have fully double flowers with no central disc of florets, so they appear to be a mass of quite broad, flat petals that are usually only slightly pointed or completely blunt at the tip. The overall size of the plants in this category also varies widely, from stocky 2 m (6–7 ft.) solid giants to compact bedding dahlias that grow to only about 38 cm (15 in.). The flowers are the archetypal dahlia flower form; most people would recognize them as dahlias in a flower-identity parade. They offer a mass of identical, never-ending petals with no visible daisy-like centre. Some types are known as formal decoratives, others informal. The difference relates to a tighter arrangement of petals or a slightly looser, more relaxed formation.

I love both types of decorative dahlia, but I tend to go for informal decoratives among other plants in borders and containers in the garden. But when it comes to cutting, the blooms of tightly packed formal decorative varieties make a good contrast with other flowers. The formals can be a total knockout on the exhibitor's show bench. For me, this is a sort of decorative dahlia nirvana, where this group comes into its own.

STELLAR DAHLIAS

Stellar dahlias are really a special form of a decorative dahlia. I'm rather fond of this group. The showy petals of the florets are cupped, almost shaped like canoes, and appear slightly swept back as they spiral out from the centre toward the edges of the bloom. They are smashing.

Genetics and Hybrids

The vast majority of dahlias cultivated in gardens all over the world are complex hybrids. Botanically they are often referred to as *Dahlia* ×*variabilis*. However, the National Dahlia Society's current thinking is that *D.* ×*hortensis* is the most appropriate Latin name. The × indicates that these plants are a hybrid cross. The original parents are some of the 36 species of dahlias found growing in Mexico.

The different species dahlias can contribute specific characteristics to the dahlia genetic pool, but over the years only a relatively small number have been used in hybridization, mainly *Dahlia coccinea* and *D. pinnata*. Recently Keith Hammett, an internationally renowned dahlia expert and plant scientist based in New Zealand, has conducted detailed studies of the genetics and chromosome numbers of dahlia species and varieties. His work has revealed that the modern hybrid varieties we've grown to love are genetically extremely complex characters, often with eight sets of chromosomes. Polyploidy, which means that each cell contains more than two sets of paired chromosomes, is extremely common in dahlia species and cultivars. Systematic studies of the genus *Dahlia* by Dale Saar at Northern Illinois University have also done much to dispel some of the myths and commonly held untruths about species dahlias, and replace them with scientific and research-based facts. Dale has carried out numerous dahlia explorations in the field in Mexico and travelled throughout the country to study wild populations growing in their natural habitat. Her website, wilddahlias.com, is a must for anyone who wants to know more about species dahlias.

Armed with this new understanding of dahlia genetics and the importance of chromosome numbers, dahlia breeders are now looking at all the original species dahlias in a new light, and are starting to back-cross different varieties in the hybridization of completely new types of dahlia. To achieve a new dahlia variety that has characteristics closer to one of its original species parents, an established garden variety is crossed with a plant of one of its parental species. The offspring or seedlings that result from this back-cross often have a genetic identity closer to that of the species parent. In some ways this can be seen as refining the breeding of a particular dahlia variety to bring it closer in line with the qualities of an original species parent.

Now that matching up chromosome numbers of individual species is understood more clearly, new crosses are being tried to introduce completely new characters to the resulting offspring. For the first time, new varieties of tree dahlias in colours other than mauve and white are being bred, and the desirable foliage characteristics of species like *Dahlia dissecta* and *D. apiculata* have been used in breeding dahlia varieties such as the Mystic series. In terms of brand-new cultivars with a long list of garden-worthy and desirable characteristics, the future for dahlias is very bright indeed.

Octoploids, DNA, and Jumping Genes: Dahlia Genetic Soup

MOST GARDEN DAHLIA varieties are octoploids, meaning they have eight sets of chromosomes. It is rare for a plant to have eight. The majority of plants are diploids, just like us, and have only two sets. Garden dahlias have lots of genes, and after years of breeding this has resulted in many different genetic combinations and variations. This has given rise to all sorts of characteristics, including colours, tones, growth habits, and forms. However, dahlias also contain many DNA sequences that can move about (known as transposons, transposable elements, or jumping genes). These factors mean that dahlias have the potential for a phenomenal amount of diversity and make them open to all kinds of mutations. These hybrid octoploid blooms are genetically very complex, unstable characters. There are thousands of different variations of dahlias, and the sheer scale of their diversity can be overwhelming for anyone new to these vivacious plants.

The Species

Naturalists and biologists define *species* as populations of organisms that have a very high level of genetic similarity. Dahlia species are plants that are genetically the same or similar to the plants found growing in the wild. However, species dahlias in cultivation often bear little resemblance to their wild cousins found in Central and South America. In cultivation, plants can easily interbreed, and many thought to be distinct species are often naturally occurring hybrids where two slightly different sub-species or types of a species have crossed to form a population of plants that are intraspecific hybrids. Stock species plants, like all dahlias, are also capable of mutations, so species plants obtained from cultivated collections can sometimes be unreliable.

In dahlias, *hybrid* is the term used for a plant that is the result of breeding between two plants of different species, two plants of different named varieties, or any combination

Dahlia coccinea

of these. *Interspecific hybrid* denotes a cross between two different dahlia species. Botanically, a named *variety* is given to a particular form or selection within a species to set these individuals apart from the main species type. There are some naturally occurring varieties of species dahlia, such as *Dahlia coccinea* var. *palmeri*, which can be found growing naturally in the wild.

The term *cultivar*, which means cultivated variety, helps distinguish a plant with characteristics that have arisen during or been perpetuated in cultivation. A cultivar is a plant or group of plants selected for desirable characteristics that can be maintained by propagation. Most garden dahlias are the result of man-made cultivation. Therefore, most popular dahlia varieties are actually cultivars. Breeders and growers develop them for their flower colour and form.

As a group of plants, dahlia species are a much simpler, subtler offering than their highly bred cultivar cousins. However, along with the ever-increasing popularity of new single dahlia varieties, their value is now being re-considered and they are being welcomed back into the garden with a new enthusiasm. I encourage any gardener to try growing species dahlias. Virtually all of them have flowers with only one single outer row of florets with slightly bigger, showier petals. Next to their bold, bright, hybrid cousins, they are decidedly delicate. This refined and subtle beauty is charming, and many of the species can make great garden plants. If you're the sort of gardener that tends to prefer simple, elegant flowers to showy hybrids, species dahlias are for you. The following are some of my favourites.

DAHLIA COCCINEA

This species is quite common in its native Mexico, and it comes in various colour forms. The plants have bright, simple flowers in shades from sunny yellows to bright oranges and reds. A lovely, velvety, ruby red form of *Dahlia coccinea* grows at Great Dixter. It is available from the National Collection in the United Kingdom and it's known as *D. coccinea* 'Mary Keen'.

My favourite form of this species, however, is *Dahlia coccinea* var. *palmeri*. It has the most wonderfully divided frothy foliage, and grows very tall, ultimately to a height of

The zingy tangerine orange bloom of *Dahlia coccinea* var. *palmeri*.

Dahlia imperialis growing at the National Collection of Dahlias in Cornwall, England.

about 2.3 m (7.5 ft.). It's a big plant, but unlike other dahlias it has a wonderful delicate habit of carefully growing through other plants. Its bright orange, simple, daisy-like flowers can seem like they appear out of nowhere. Plant it among tall grasses such as *Miscanthus*, purple *Verbena bonariensis*, and raspberry *Knautia macedonica* for full floaty effect. Note that very young plants do not show up the dissected leaf as well as older plants.

DAHLIA DISSECTA

The cut leaf dahlia—or, as I affectionately call it, the fairy dahlia—is a delicate, pretty little thing, and very lovable. Simple, single flowers, often pure white and sometimes pale lavender, sit on dark slender, arching stems above a sea of the most amazing dainty, frothy foliage. It's another Mexican dahlia species, but this one grows high up in mountainous regions and doesn't like conditions that are too hot or too wet. Let it dry out slightly between watering. The plant grows to a height of about 90 cm (36 in.), but it is more likely to be as short as 30 cm (12 in.) if you grow it in a container, as I do. I've seen pictures of it growing as a delicate, medium-height ground cover at the front of borders. In addition to its dwarf characteristics, this species has the most deeply and finely dissected glossy green leaves. It looks elegant grown on its own in a terra-cotta pot, and it will do fine in very light shade. It's adorable.

DAHLIA IMPERIALIS

This is one of a number of species of tree dahlia, and another native of Mexico. Both the straight species and the white flowering 'Alba' are absolute giants. This plant often

Dahlia imperialis

Dahlia dissecta

reaches more that 6 m (20 ft.) in the wild. It has very large, glaucous, lush green leaves, and thick, bamboo-like stems. Its flowers are produced in large clusters at the tips of the tall stems, and they are quite large, though simple and elegant, with colours that range from lavender through to white. The individual blooms are often about 10 to 15 cm (4–6 in.) across, and their single ray of large drooping petals has a subtle, tissue paper–like texture.

The Aztecs called this dahlia *acocotli*, meaning water cane. They valued the plant as a source of water for traveling hunters. Tree dahlias store large reserves of water in their stems, so they quickly succumb to hard frosts. In areas where early frosts occur, *Dahlia imperialis* will probably not bloom before the dormant season. It's well worth trying to grow one in a pot, as it will look fabulous and will impress your neighbours. It is not likely to flower, but its size, foliage, habit, and tropical silhouette is fantastic enough on its own. Place this dahlia in a huge pot and put it in your warmest, sunniest, most sheltered spot. When it's growing, feed sparingly but often. Keep the plant well watered, too; it is thirsty and grows quickly. I have read that this dahlia must be in the ground to grow properly and bloom well. However, I have grown it successfully in a large 75-litre (20-gallon) black plastic pot next to a south-facing wall in a virtually frost-free communal garden in London. It was in flower on Christmas Day.

DAHLIA MERCKII

Dahlia merckii is another dainty dahlia, but it is much taller than *D. dissecta*. It can be quite spindly as a young plant, almost feeble in appearance. However, if you like your plants on the looser, wilder side, you will likely be a fan. I can't help rather liking it myself. Once it gets established it will form quite a big clump, and then overall it doesn't seem quite as gawky. The flower stems are long, tall, and elegant. It's very floriferous, producing a huge amount of simple, starry blooms that are white and pale lavender to pink-purple, about 5 to 10 cm (2–4 in.) across, so quite small. It grows best scrambling among plants like purple *Verbena bonariensis*, tall pink-and-white annual *Cosmos bipinnatus*, and *Calamagrostis* grass. The flowers look like dancing dahlia butterflies.

Dahlia sherffii

DAHLIA SHERFFII

Dahlia sherffii hails from northern Mexico. The plants have very long, slender stems supporting rather elegant single flowers high above the foliage. The blooms are about 7 to 9 cm (3–3.5 in.) across and have petals ranging pink to lilac to lavender, with a small central disc of golden florets. Sometimes you can also spot a small area of yellow at the base of each petal. It's a very tall, herbaceous species that grows to about 140 cm (55 in.), and has long, narrow, dark green leaflets compared to most garden cultivars. It's quite a sprawling plant, so a bit like *D. merckii*, and it's a good idea to grow it among other plants for some support. I love the *D. sherffii* plants that I grow, but knowing the dubious nature of species plants in cultivation, I am not entirely sure that they are representative of the true species. Many of the wild species have multiple sets of chromosomes and, like garden cultivars, can be genetically unstable and readily hybridize with other plants.

DAHLIA TENUICAULIS

Another tree dahlia from Mexico, but not so widely grown, is *Dahlia tenuicaulis*. It is an ever-blooming plant, with flowers appearing almost year-round when it reaches a mature size. The flowers are more of a pink-purple and about 8 cm (3 in.) wide. As with other tree dahlias, it has bamboo-like main stems. Growing the plant in a large pot can help limit its size, but in my experience that doesn't stop the plants from flowering.

This tree dahlia can be evergreen in frost-free areas or if grown in a greenhouse or conservatory. However, it will die down and go dormant just like other dahlias if grown in colder environments. It's not quite the towering monster that *Dahlia imperialis* can be, and has a slightly bushier, more branching habit. This plant can be a 4.5 m (15 ft.) high by 2.5 m (8 ft.) wide giant in frost-free locations. The blooms have a very delicate fragrance and can appear quite early in the season, but the grandest show of flower comes later in the autumn and winter months.

Dahlia merckii

I rather like the dark purple colour of the young fresh foliage of *Dahlia tenuicaulis*, as well as its slightly hairy, nettle-like texture.

I adore the apricot and coral pink colour of the blooms of this plant of *Dahlia sherffii* in my garden, but I'm not entirely convinced it's true to the species type. I have a hunch it could be a hybrid, possibly *D. sherffii* × *D. coccinea* or *D. sherffii* × *D. merckii*. The jury's out.

Dahlia tenuicaulis

200 VARIETIES FOR THE GARDEN

When it comes to recommending great garden dahlias, it's hard to know where to begin. There are thousands upon thousands of wonderful varieties, and anyone who loves unashamedly vivid and vibrant flowers risks becoming addicted to the colour rush. You have been warned.

Colour is king in my garden, so I have organized the dahlia selections in colour groupings. I've picked out personal favourites that grow really well in a garden setting, be it in mixed herbaceous borders, container displays, bedding schemes, or traditional dahlia beds. I have also included varieties that are a mix of different colours in the same bloom, known as blends or bicolours. These are grouped according to the dominant colour of the bloom.

The fun of growing dahlias is that every year, just when you think you've found your absolute favourite varieties, you discover new ones and your collection keeps growing and evolving. This guide will hopefully provide you with a good base from which to begin. But the fun really starts when you explore the trial grounds, nurseries, and gardens of specialist dahlia growers and breeders. Then you are off following your own yellow brick road toward some very enjoyable and daring dahlia adventures. Note that height and spread measurements in the descriptions are approximations of the size of a one-year-old plant grown in good garden conditions. Each variety's unique selling points and garden worthiness are also open to some debate, but I have listed the reasons why I choose to grow them and why I think you should too. Before we look at the plants themselves, let's look at the colour wheel.

Dahlia 'Dovegrove'

The Colour Wheel

It can be a challenge to clearly describe some of the incredible colours and how they interplay within a dahlia bloom. A basic understanding of the colour wheel can help to explain how different colours work, both with each other and when blended together.

Hue and colour are basically the same thing. When referring to a red or a burgundy dahlia, the pure, true colour or hue is red. So *hue* refers to the original foundation colour. *Shades* are the pure colour or hue with a degree of black added to darken. *Tints* are the pure colour or hue with a degree of white added to lighten. *Tones* are the pure colour or hue with a degree of grey (both black and white) added to tone down the hue.

We all know the primary colours (red, yellow, and blue), as well as the secondary colours (orange, green, and purple) made by combinations of these pure hues. A lot of the fun with dahlias starts between the primary and secondary colours. Some of the best dahlia varieties inhabit these tertiary colour areas, such as yellow-orange, red-orange, red-purple, blue-purple. Colours like pink are often incredibly complex. Dahlias come in shades of pink with elements of red, blue, yellow, orange, grey, cream, and white. They are all pink, but each is quite different from the next.

Don't be flummoxed by colour. We all see colours differently. They are just our brains' interpretations of the way light bounces off an object. In dahlias, colours we all think we know and understand can become very exciting. The American Dahlia Society recognizes 225 different colours and offers a guide to help navigate through all the main groups. But if you put three dahlia experts together and ask them to describe a bloom's colour in detail, you will likely get three very contrasting responses.

The descriptions that follow are largely based on what I've noted while growing the plants myself, although I have referenced official accounts of colour in catalogues and on the websites of breeders and collectors. Sometimes varieties described as red look decidedly orange to my eyes, and some pinks seem closer to magenta or purple.

Considering the number of genes that could be involved in the flower development of an octoploid dahlia

Dahlia 'Black Tucker'

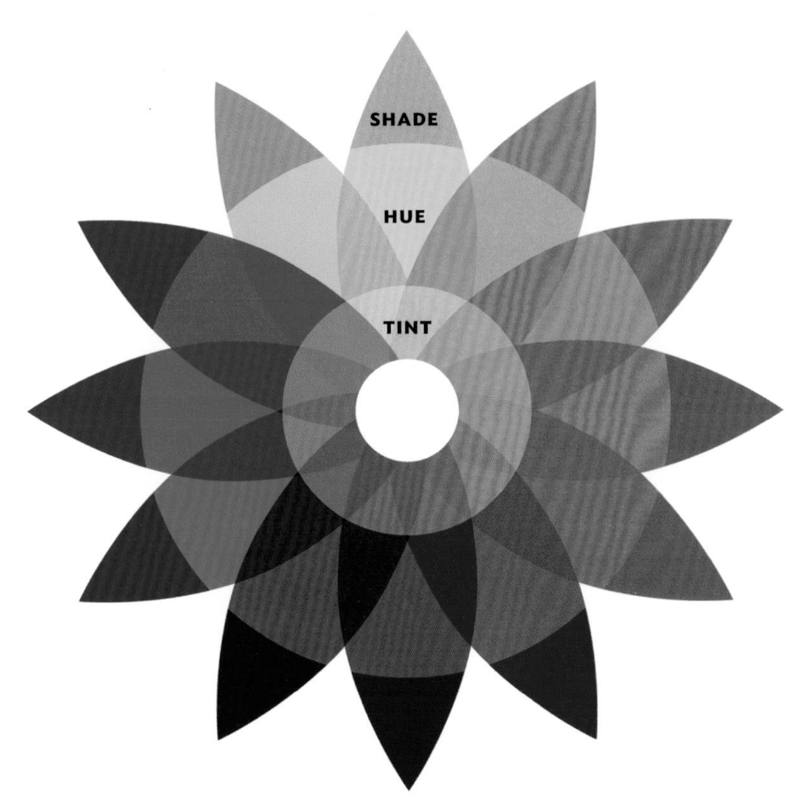

variety, it is no wonder the range of resulting colours, tints, tones, shades, blends, and bicolours is not only glorious, but potentially mind boggling. However, it's more complex than just genetics. The acidity or alkalinity of the soil in which a plant is growing can affect the appearance of the pigments in the flower petals. UV light may influence colour too. The primary pigment that dahlia petals contain often determines the main colour of the flower, but petals can contain mixes of several different pigments. Anthocyanins are often the class of pigment responsible for the incredible colour range of dahlia petals.

If a dahlia is put under considerable stress from outside factors like drought, over-watering, insect infestation, UV light, or a lack of appropriate fertilizer, these factors may influence a change in the expression of the flower colour. Anything that can adversely affect the plant's ability to synthesize the correct amounts of pigment can also cause the plant's overall flower colour to change.

Dahlias cultivated in cooler climates can have deeper, more vibrant colours than the same varieties growing in a warmer climate. Plants in full sun may have more flowers, but of a paler colour. I find that the intensity of a flower colour is often strongly linked to the availability of the right nutrients, at the right time, combined with how much strong, direct sun a bloom has experienced. Under-fertilized plants tell you they need more food by offering up pale, lacklustre blooms. The flowers of some varieties fade more than others as they develop, if planted in very exposed sunny locations.

CLARET, BURGUNDY, AND MAROON

If you want to inject depth and drama into a flowerbed, you can't go wrong with dark, velvety reds in sumptuous shades and tantalizing tones reminiscent of the deepest, richest red wines. Some offer hints of blackberry, raspberry, and cranberry; others have a crimson blush or chocolate overtone. They are completely delicious and ever so slightly devilish. Drink them in.

'Bishop of Auckland'

This completely glorious variety is arguably the best of the Bishop series, with velvety crimson petals, dark centres, superbly simple single flowers, and deep green-black foliage.

WHAT TYPE? Single
HOW TALL? 90 cm (36 in.)
WHAT SPREAD? 60 cm (24 in.)
WHY GROW IT? Great cut flower, perfect for pollinators, great for container growing, great garden dahlia

'Sam Hopkins'

A beautiful black velveteen decorative variety with stunning buds. It is one of the biggest black dahlia varieties and it becomes quite a substantial plant.

WHAT TYPE? Decorative
HOW TALL? 120 cm (47 in.)
WHAT SPREAD? 70 cm (28 in.)
WHY GROW IT? Great cut flower

'Chat Noir'

What's not to love about the black cat, a wonderful velvety red semi-cactus with long stems? The prominent lime green flower bracts also add extra character to the centre of the blooms of this superb semi-cactus variety.

WHAT TYPE? Semi-cactus
HOW TALL? 140 cm (55 in.)
WHAT SPREAD? 80 cm (32 in.)
WHY GROW IT? Great cut flower, great vase life

'Karma Choc'▲

Mirror, mirror on the wall, who is the darkest one of all? This velvety waterlily has stems that are just as dark as its incredible blooms. It may reach only the height of the tallest dwarf, but it could still bring Snow White and the Evil Queen to their knees. I'm spellbound.

WHAT TYPE? Waterlily
HOW TALL? 75 cm (30 in.)
WHAT SPREAD? 50 cm (20 in.)
WHY GROW IT? Great cut flower, great for containers, great vase life

'Lights Out'▲

This outstanding, versatile, vigorous medium-size velvety black decorative is great for growing in herbaceous borders, both as a cut flower and in containers.

WHAT TYPE? Decorative
HOW TALL? 110 cm (43 in.)
WHAT SPREAD? 60 cm (24 in.)
WHY GROW IT? Great all-around variety, great cut flower, great border variety

'Arabian Night'▸

This charming, deep claret, small-flowered decorative is all-around great. Like 'Chat Noir', it has small green floral bracts in the centre of the bloom that add an interesting dimension to the flowers.

WHAT TYPE? Decorative
HOW TALL? 110 cm (43 in.)
WHAT SPREAD? 60 cm (24 in.)
WHY GROW IT? Great all-around variety, great cut flower, great border variety

'Nuit d'Eté' ▲

From an Arabian night to a frisky French summer evening. This devilishly dark red semi-cactus is a rival to 'Chat Noir'. It's very slightly more spiky and sea urchin–like.

WHAT TYPE? Semi-cactus
HOW TALL? 140 cm (55 in.)
WHAT SPREAD? 80 cm (32 in.)
WHY GROW IT? Great cut flower, great tall border variety

'Mexican Black' ▼

An unusual and mysterious dahlia. Often sold as *Cosmos* × *Dahlia* 'Mexican Black', so a hybrid between a Cosmos and a Dahlia is suggested, although I'm reliably informed such crosses aren't possible. Perhaps this is just a single dahlia that looks very much like *Cosmos atrosanguineus*. Whatever its genetics, it has the most fabulous nodding scented flowers above pleasant dark green pinnate foliage. The individual blooms are single and deepest, darkest red-black with contrasting big golden centres. I first saw this wonderful plant at Cotswold Garden Flowers in England, and to quote the equally wonderful proprietor Bob Brown, like most dahlias, "It responds well to good living."

WHAT TYPE? Single
HOW TALL? 75 cm (30 in.)
WHAT SPREAD? 40 cm (16 in.)
WHY GROW IT? Great for containers, great border variety, perfect for pollinators

'Black Satin'

This deep red-black formal decorative with 10 cm (4 in.) diameter blooms is a good, solid, prolific variety that produces lots and lots of stems. It's perfect for cutting or in the border, and it provides sultry satin chic blooms.

WHAT TYPE? Formal decorative
HOW TALL? 153 cm (60 in.)
WHAT SPREAD? 90 cm (36 in.)
WHY GROW IT? Great cut flower, great border variety, strong flower form

'Rip City' ▸

'Rip City' is a truly gorgeous black-crimson dahlia; a vigorous, lush-growing semi-cactus, bordering on an informal decorative dahlia, with wonderful wavy petals. 'Ripples' ▾ is a sport, or colour mutation, of 'Rip City', with a slightly bigger bloom and a more velvety purple persuasion. Both are complete knockouts as cut flowers or tall, back-of-the-border dahlias.

WHAT TYPE? Semi-cactus
HOW TALL? 137 cm (54 in.)
WHAT SPREAD? 80 cm (32 in.)
WHY GROW THEM? Great border varieties, great cut flowers

'Rock Star'

The blackberry wine, red-purple pincushion blooms of this anemone are wonderful. The way the tips of the outer ring of petals fade slightly to raspberry at the edge and are slightly swept back toward the stem is just lovely.

WHAT TYPE? Anemone
HOW TALL? 120 cm (47 in.)
WHAT SPREAD? 70 cm (28 in.)
WHY GROW IT? Great border variety, great for containers, unusual colour combination

'Tahoma Moonshot'

A unique and striking star dahlia that is great in the garden. It has wacky black windmill blooms about 8 cm (3 in.) across with glowing yellow centres. If you're naturally drawn to the unusual, you'll probably adore it.

WHAT TYPE? Star
HOW TALL? 107 cm (42 in.)
WHAT SPREAD? 50 cm (20 in.)
WHY GROW IT? Great border variety, perfect for pollinators, unusual form

'La Recoleta'

Quite a new dark blackberry dahlia that I first encountered at the dahlia trials at the Royal Horticultural Society gardens at Wisley. Its tight, perfectly formed, ball-shaped flowers are about 7.5 cm (3 in.) across and purple-black in bud before turning ruby-black. Mesmerizing.

WHAT TYPE? Decorative
HOW TALL? 75 cm (30 in.)
WHAT SPREAD? 70 cm (28 in.)
WHY GROW IT? Great cut flower, good compact garden variety, stunning colour

'Soulman'

This shaggy, relaxed, ruby-black anemone dahlia has been one of my favourites for years. I love its divided foliage, and overall it's a handsome plant that looks good in the border or in a pot. You gotta have soul.

WHAT TYPE? Anemone
HOW TALL? 100 cm (40 in.)
WHAT SPREAD? 50 cm (20 in.)
WHY GROW IT? Great for borders or containers, unusual form, good foliage

'Inglebrook Jill'

A deepest double raspberry red collerette. It's absolutely gorgeous and one of my very favourite collerettes to grow in the garden. Bees and butterflies love it, and it's a great cut flower too.

WHAT TYPE? Collerette
HOW TALL? 128 cm (50 in.)
WHAT SPREAD? 80 cm (32 in.)
WHY GROW IT? Great cut flower, great border variety, perfect for pollinators

'Twyning's Chocolate'

A clean and crisp chocolate-red single bred by the talented Mark Twyning at the National Collection of Dahlias in Cornwall, England. It has good lightly bronzed green foliage and lots of sultry flowers. Tasty.

WHAT TYPE? Single
HOW TALL? 120 cm (47 in.)
WHAT SPREAD? 60 cm (24 in.)
WHY GROW IT? Great border variety, perfect for pollinators, great for containers

'Dovegrove'

A rich, velvety, blood red single dahlia raised by international dahlia breeder and guru Keith Hammett. It's a handsome plant with purple-red flower stems and deep green-black foliage. Great in borders and containers, and a brilliant garden variety. Winner of a Royal Horticultural Society Award of Garden Merit.

WHAT TYPE? Single
HOW TALL? 140 cm (55 in.)
WHAT SPREAD? 80 cm (32 in.)
WHY GROW IT? Great garden variety, perfect for pollinators, good for containers

'Hillcrest Regal'

A magnificent maroon-red collerette with tiny flecks of white on the tips of the inner collar petals that light up the bloom. Great for the garden and for cutting. Winner of a Royal Horticultural Society Award of Garden Merit.

WHAT TYPE? Collerette
HOW TALL? 110 cm (43 in.)
WHAT SPREAD? 60 cm (24 in.)
WHY GROW IT? Great garden variety, great cut flower, perfect for pollinators

'Chee'

This very dark, velvety, plum-red waterlily is a large, impressive, floriferous variety with dark green foliage.

WHAT TYPE? Waterlily
HOW TALL? 120 cm (47 in.)
WHAT SPREAD? 60 cm (24 in.)
WHY GROW IT? Great cut flower, good tall border variety

RED

Nothing packs a punch quite like a well-placed red dahlia, and in any sub-tropical or jungle-theme planting scheme, they're in their element. Finding truly pure red dahlia varieties can be a challenge. To my eyes, many listed as red are closer to a zingy tangerine orange, or they have a ruby, raspberry, or magenta flavour. I've endeavoured to choose super scarlets, vivacious vermilions, and the hottest and reddest of the reds in this selection. But overall I've included reds—in all their various different tints, tones, and shades—that collectively bring heat and lots of va-va-voom to the party.

'Happy Single Romeo' ◂

A deep wine-red dwarf single, with dark foliage. This is a pretty fabulous and versatile plant. I'm particularly fond of the Happy Single series, which is just one of an ever-increasing range of small dahlias being produced as perfect playmates for tiny gardens and patio pots.

WHAT TYPE? Single
HOW TALL? 80 cm (32 in.)
WHAT SPREAD? 30 cm (12 in.)
WHY GROW IT? Great for containers, perfect for pollinators, great for small gardens and patios

'Bishop of Llandaff'▶

This is *the* classic garden dahlia variety and an icon in the dahlia revolution. It's hard to fault this brilliant red semi-double peony and its fantastic frothy, deepest black foliage. I've grown it for years and still adore it. I've also grown a number that are quite similar, such as 'Tally Ho'▶ (winner of a Royal Horticultural Society Award of Garden Merit) and 'Japanese Bishop'▲, which are also good varieties, but the foliage of 'Bishop of Llandaff' gives it the edge. Winner of a Royal Horticultural Society Award of Garden Merit.

WHAT TYPE? Peony/semi-double
HOW TALL? 100 cm (40 in.)
WHAT SPREAD? 50 cm (20 in.)
WHY GROW IT? Great garden variety, perfect for pollinators, great foliage

'Grenadier'

One of my absolute favourite red dahlias. This small- to medium-flowered decorative variety has fully double blooms with broad, flat, blunt-tipped petals. Their arrangement on the bloom reminds me of fussy breast feathers on a show pigeon. It has good dark green foliage that's darker when more light gets to it, and blooms held on long, elegant stems. It's just delicious. Winner of a Royal Horticultural Society Award of Garden Merit.

WHAT TYPE? Informal decorative
HOW TALL? 100 cm (40 in.)
WHAT SPREAD? 70 cm (28 in.)
WHY GROW IT? Great border variety, great foliage, elegant habit, good cut flower

'American Beauty'

It was love at first sight when I encountered this variety, with ravishingly red ruffled petals, at Swan Island Dahlias near Portland, Oregon. The blooms are about 15 cm (6 in.) across. It's a very handsome plant with strong upright stems and good glossy, deep green foliage too.

WHAT TYPE? Informal decorative
HOW TALL? 122 cm (48 in.)
WHAT SPREAD? 80 cm (32 in.)
WHY GROW IT? Great garden variety, great exhibition variety, strong robust plant

'Baby Red'

This perfect lilliput dahlia flowers its socks off; it's hard to keep up with dead-heading. It's a smart, perky plant that is perfect for containers and window boxes, with red daisy flowers that appear early and are only about 4 cm (1.5 in.) across. An adorable little devil.

WHAT TYPE? Mignon single
HOW TALL? 30 cm (12 in.)
WHAT SPREAD? 30 cm (12 in.)
WHY GROW IT? Great garden variety, perfect for pollinators, great for containers and window boxes

'Mars'

A bright and jolly red collerette that has both a red collar and red petals with a golden yellow centre. The individual blooms are around 12 cm (5 in.) across. The slightly curled pointed petals are rather funky too.

WHAT TYPE? Collerette
HOW TALL? 122 cm (48 in.)
WHAT SPREAD? 50 cm (20 in.)
WHY GROW IT? Great garden variety, perfect for pollinators

'Honka Red' ▲

Most of the Honka varieties are great, but 'Honka Red' has to be my favourite. It has rich red windmill blooms that, like all star or single orchids, look great en masse. 'Marie Schnugg' ▶ is a very similar variety, and I find them hard to tell apart. Both are top notch and really fun to grow. Both are winners of a Royal Horticultural Society Award of Garden Merit.

WHAT TYPE? Single orchid
HOW TALL? 80 cm (32 in.)
WHAT SPREAD? 50 cm (20 in.)
WHY GROW THEM? Great garden varieties, perfect for pollinators, quirky flower form

'Edwin's Sunset'▲

I've recently fallen for this stand-out berry red water-lily variety, which has stunning blooms on strong, vigorous upright growth. It's a great variety for the exhibitor's bench, and arguably more an exhibition dahlia than a garden variety. Nonetheless it's wonderful to grow as a cut flower or for a prominent place in a big border to make a dramatic statement. Winner of a Royal Horticultural Society Award of Garden Merit.

WHAT TYPE? Waterlily
HOW TALL? 140 cm (55 in.)
WHAT SPREAD? 90 cm (36 in.)
WHY GROW IT? Great cut flower, total diva, great exhibition variety

'Chimborazo'▼

If you need a touch of the exotic, 'Chimborazo' can bring a carnival atmosphere to a planting combination. It's a lively concoction of deep claret red petals and a creamy yellow collar, and the blooms sit on long elegant stems. 'Kaiser Walter'▶ is a similar dramatic variety that I also love. Flora exotica.

WHAT TYPE? Collerette
HOW TALL? 100 cm (40 in.)
WHAT SPREAD? 50 cm (20 in.)
WHY GROW THEM? Total Mardi Gras, great garden varieties, perfect for pollinators

'Christmas Carol'▾

'Christmas Carol' and 'Heartthrob' ◂ are two brilliant compact varieties that are similar to 'Chimborazo' but lean slightly nearer to red-orange or burnt orange. They are slightly shorter, so great container varieties, floriferous, and full of energy.

WHAT TYPE? Collerette
HOW TALL? 70 cm (28 in.)
WHAT SPREAD? 30 cm (12 in.)
WHY GROW THEM? Great for containers, great garden varieties, perfect for pollinators

'Wittemans Superba'

This is an impressive small to medium-size red semi-cactus that instantly brings to mind the gardens of Great Dixter. It's a take-no-prisoners variety that is totally glorious but a complete diva. Great cut flower, great spot plant that adds drama to a mixed border or tropical planting scheme. I predict a riot. Winner of a Royal Horticultural Society Award of Garden Merit.

WHAT TYPE? Semi-cactus
HOW TALL? 140 cm (55 in.)
WHAT SPREAD? 90 cm (36 in.)
WHY GROW IT? Great cut flower, total diva

'Comet'◂

'Comet' is a rich deep cranberry crimson anemone that I met on my first visit to the National Collection of Dahlias in Cornwall, England. It's otherworldly and works wonderfully well in containers. 'Scarlet Comet' ▾ is a brighter vermilion red version with a much smaller central pincushion that I assume is either a sport of 'Comet', or vice versa.

WHAT TYPE? Anemone
HOW TALL? 75 cm (30 in.)
WHAT SPREAD? 40 cm (16 in.)
WHY GROW THEM? Great container varieties, great border varieties, rich colours

'Weston Pirate'▾

A dark cranberry red cactus dahlia that's great for the garden. The blooms are smallish, but you get lots of them on a tall, elegant plant. I particularly love the tiny yellow stigmas that protrude at the base of the florets. Divine. Winner of a Royal Horticultural Society Award of Garden Merit.

WHAT TYPE? Cactus
HOW TALL? 120 cm (47 in.)
WHAT SPREAD? 60 cm (24 in.)
WHY GROW IT? Great garden dahlia, great cut flower

'Ann Breckenfelder'▲

There are many really great shocking red collerette varieties that have a wildly contrasting collar of petals, but 'Ann Breckenfelder' is one of the most confident I've ever come across. This is a quality plant with great overall stature, crisp clean blooms, and good green foliage. She's a knockout. Winner of a Royal Horticultural Society Award of Garden Merit.

WHAT TYPE? Collerette
HOW TALL? 120 cm (47 in.)
WHAT SPREAD? 60 cm (24 in.)
WHY GROW IT? Great garden dahlia, great cut flower, perfect for pollinators

'Copper Queen'▶

'Copper Queen' is a fantastic border or container variety with deep dark foliage and rusty chocolate-red fully double decorative blooms. It's a great variety to try in containers with lots of different types of glossy dark green, acid green, and variegated-leaved plants.

WHAT TYPE? Decorative
HOW TALL? 120 cm (47 in.)
WHAT SPREAD? 60 cm (24 in.)
WHY GROW IT? Great garden dahlia, great for containers, good foliage

'Bloodstone' ◂

I'm very fond of 'Bloodstone' and 'Murdoch' ▾, two quite similar, small-flowered decorative varieties. Both are a rich, true, bright London-bus red and rather wonderful. These are almost waterlily in flower shape, but not quite. The form of both, however, is perfection. They have elegant, long stems, so they need support, but they're worth it.

WHAT TYPE? Decorative
HOW TALL? 120 cm (47 in.)
WHAT SPREAD? 60 cm (24 in.)
WHY GROW THEM? Great garden dahlias, great herbaceous border dahlias, good green foliage

'Trelyn Crimson' ▾

Possibly the most truly crimson scarlet collerette I've ever seen. It's a wonderful Santa's suit red. Not the easiest of colours to combine in a border, but a brilliant variety and a handsome plant. Bedazzling.

WHAT TYPE? Collerette
HOW TALL? 120 cm (47 in.)
WHAT SPREAD? 60 cm (24 in.)
WHY GROW IT? Great garden dahlia, great herbaceous border dahlia, perfect for pollinators, knockout colour

'Hootenanny'

A strong cherry red collerette with a really dark bronze central eye of florets and a collar that's blushed with white. Good dark green foliage and dark red-brown stems on a handsome robust plant. A great variety for arrangements, but cut young blooms while the centres have a tight, waxy appearance.

WHAT TYPE? Collerette
HOW TALL? 122 cm (48 in.)
WHAT SPREAD? 50 cm (20 in.)
WHY GROW IT? Great container variety, good garden variety, good cut flower

ORANGE

I'm growing more and more orange dahlia varieties. I think it's a colour you grow to either love or hate. I began my dahlia obsession with a cactus variety called 'Banker', which is often listed as red, but to me it's a deep, intense tangerine. There are some amazingly strong orange dahlia cultivars, and when grown among deep pink, magenta, claret, and raspberry red varieties, they can steal the display with their zestfulness. I could probably write a whole book about orange dahlias, so picking my favourites has been rather difficult. I can assure you that I adore the ones I've chosen, but there are so many more orange varieties out there that would also be brilliant.

'Totally Tangerine'

A new find and an instant favourite. I'm becoming more and more enthralled by anemone dahlias, and this one is fantastic. It's a neat, compact plant with gentle orange blooms about 7 cm (3 in.) wide that have a rosy reverse to the underside of the petals. The central pincushion of florets is a rusty deep orange with golden throats. Totally charming.

WHAT TYPE? Anemone
HOW TALL? 90 cm (36 in.)
WHAT SPREAD? 50 cm (20 in.)
WHY GROW IT? Great garden variety, great cut flower, good compact container variety

'Banker'▸

'Banker' is my very favourite deep tangerine orange cactus. It's just stunning. I love the gentle golden sport 'Amber Banker' ▾ almost as much. Both are great cut flower varieties, and their medium to large blooms look amazing used as floating flowers inside big spherical vases. Let the fireworks commence.

WHAT TYPE? Cactus
HOW TALL? 130 cm (51 in.)
WHAT SPREAD? 70 cm (28 in.)
WHY GROW THEM? Great cut flowers, total divas

'Giraffe'▾

This is a pale orange double orchid dahlia with an unusual stripy reverse to the twisted petals, which gives the bloom a very jazzy appearance. I know it's not for everyone, but I have a soft spot for the extraordinary. It doesn't get too tall, so it's great for pots and all sorts of containers.

WHAT TYPE? Double orchid
HOW TALL? 40 cm (16 in.)
WHAT SPREAD? 30 cm (12 in.)
WHY GROW IT? Very unusual, great garden variety, good container variety

'Orange Pathfinder' ◀

There are a number of medium-size single and peony/semi-double varieties available that have strong orange flowers with dark centres and gorgeous dark foliage. 'Orange Pathfinder' is probably my favourite, closely followed by 'Bishop of Oxford' ▼ and 'Catherine Deneuve' ▲. On the whole there is little to distinguish between them. All three varieties have vibrant orange blooms, flower prolifically, and are excellent garden dahlias. They also look fantastic in containers, and the bees go mad for them.

WHAT TYPE? Peony/semi-double
HOW TALL? 70 cm (28 in.)
WHAT SPREAD? 40 cm (16 in.)
WHY GROW THEM? Great garden varieties, good for containers, perfect for pollinators, great dark foliage

'David Howard'

A classic bronze orange decorative dahlia with the perfect combination of delicious dark coppery foliage. It's a great sturdy variety that doesn't need much staking or support, and it looks amazing planted among deep blue *Salvia guaranitica* and *Verbena bonariensis*. Winner of a Royal Horticultural Society Award of Garden Merit.

WHAT TYPE? Decorative
HOW TALL? 75 cm (30 in.)
WHAT SPREAD? 40 cm (16 in.)
WHY GROW IT? Great garden variety, good container variety, great dark bronze foliage

‘Jescot Julie’▲

Two double orchid dahlias that I love. ‘Jescot Julie’ has fiery bright orange petals that have a darker, almost plum-coloured, reverse and lush bright green foliage. It’s a stand-out cut-flower variety and, with support, looks fabulous in the garden too. ‘Julie One’ ▼ is similar, but the petal contrast is pale amber orange with rusty red on the reverse, and the foliage is a much darker green. The petals and blooms of both varieties bring to mind an exotic bird of paradise.

WHAT TYPE? Double orchid
HOW TALL? 120 cm (47 in.)
WHAT SPREAD? 60 cm (24 in.)
WHY GROW THEM? Great cut flowers, good tall border varieties, unusual petal colour contrasts, good green foliage

‘Crazy Legs’▲

‘Crazy Legs’ and her bigger brother, ‘Gitts Crazy’ ▼, are stellar dahlias with petals that contrast in colour on either side, similar to ‘Jescot Julie’ and ‘Julie One’. This time the contrast is slightly paler, more of an apricot orange with a burnt orange reverse. Both varieties flower prolifically. ‘Crazy Legs’ grows to around 122 cm (48 in.) and has compact blooms around 8 cm (3 in.) wide. ‘Gitts Crazy’ is a taller, bigger plant and has larger, more rounded blooms around 18 cm (7 in.) across. I’m becoming more and more keen on stellar types, and these two brilliant varieties are prolific bloomers and have good green foliage.

WHAT TYPE? Stellar
HOW TALL? 168 cm (66 in.)
WHAT SPREAD? 80 cm (32 in.)
WHY GROW THEM? Great cut flowers, good tall border varieties, unusual petal colour contrasts, good green foliage, great flower form

'Moonfire'

Such a classic single variety and, along with 'Bishop of Llandaff', an absolute must for anyone new to growing dahlias. It has golden orange petals that turn red-orange toward the centre, and a dark chocolate disc that glows with flecks of bright golden yellow stamens, plus bronze foliage. Looks stunning planted among lime green foliage plants. Winner of a Royal Horticultural Society Award of Garden Merit.

WHAT TYPE? Single
HOW TALL? 85 cm (34 in.)
WHAT SPREAD? 40 cm (16 in.)
WHY GROW IT? Great garden variety, great for containers, perfect for pollinators, good dark foliage

'Scura'

An adorable tiny dwarf lilliput dahlia. The blooms are perfect single dahlia daisies in brilliant deep tangerine orange with dark orange centres. 'Scura' has flowers only about 3 cm (1 in.) in diameter. Brilliant in all sorts of containers and has great green black foliage, and it flowers like crazy for months too.

WHAT TYPE? Single
HOW TALL? 50 cm (20 in.)
WHAT SPREAD? 25 cm (10 in.)
WHY GROW IT? Great for containers, perfect for pollinators, good dark foliage

'Happy Halloween'

If you love strong orange, you must have this perfect pumpkin orange decorative dahlia. It's a great cut flower variety and a strong, vigorous plant. It needs support but looks good among tall, late summer–flowering asters and tall grasses.

WHAT TYPE? Decorative
HOW TALL? 110 cm (43 in.)
WHAT SPREAD? 50 cm (20 in.)
WHY GROW IT? Great cut flower, total diva, strong colour

'Hugh Mather'

A really floriferous, well-proportioned orange waterlily with long, dark stems, lots of small flowers around 12 cm (5 in.) wide, and good dark green foliage. It's great for the herbaceous border and for cutting.

WHAT TYPE? Waterlily
HOW TALL? 140 cm (55 in.)
WHAT SPREAD? 50 cm (20 in.)
WHY GROW IT? Great cut flower, great for herbaceous borders, handsome plant

'Peach Brandy'

Another gorgeous orange waterlily on a slightly shorter plant, around 90 cm (36 in.) tall, so better for containers and smaller gardens. It has good bright green foliage.

WHAT TYPE? Waterlily
HOW TALL? 90 cm (36 in.)
WHAT SPREAD? 40 cm (16 in.)
WHY GROW IT? Great garden dahlia, good for containers, subtle colour

'Brandaris'▼

I rather love the flame orange and yellow blend of this dahlia. It's a medium semi-cactus but has the light, open feel almost of a slender-petalled waterlily. It has good dark green foliage, long dark stems, and copious flowers, but it's quite a big plant. Fabulous for cutting.

WHAT TYPE? Semi-cactus
HOW TALL? 140 cm (55 in.)
WHAT SPREAD? 60 cm (24 in.)
WHY GROW IT? Great cut flower, great for tall herbaceous border

'Bed Head'▲

I can't help but love this quirky cactus. It has a swirling mass of vibrant orange-quilled petals that won't behave. The blooms are about 10 cm (4 in.) across on very long stems. It's a good, strong, tall robust plant with good green foliage.

WHAT TYPE? Cactus
HOW TALL? 152 cm (60 in.)
WHAT SPREAD? 70 cm (28 in.)
WHY GROW IT? Great cut flower, great for herbaceous border, unusual flower form

'E Z Duzzit'

A mellow orange collerette with soft orange petals and pale orange collar. It's a great plant for the garden and has lots of gorgeous blooms for cutting. Good height for a large container or herbaceous border.

WHAT TYPE? Collerette
HOW TALL? 122 cm (48 in.)
WHAT SPREAD? 50 cm (20 in.)
WHY GROW IT? Great cut flower, good for large containers, good garden dahlia, perfect for pollinators

'Mardy Gras'▼

Fire-bright orange petals are made even more vibrant by their blend into brilliant gold at the centre of the blooms of 'Mardy Gras'. This is a perky, medium-size formal decorative dahlia that blooms approximately 6 cm (2.5 in.) across. An excellent cut-flower variety that really pops in arrangements.

WHAT TYPE? Formal decorative
HOW TALL? 122 cm (48 in.)
WHAT SPREAD? 50 cm (20 in.)
WHY GROW IT? Great cut flower, good garden dahlia, unusual colour combination

'Dream Seeker'▼

A gorgeous coral orange collerette that I saw on a stand at the Royal Horticultural Society's Tatton Park Show. It has a rosy pink collar, a delicious dark central disc, and really glossy dark bronze foliage. It's perfect for containers and all sorts of garden situations.

WHAT TYPE? Collerette
HOW TALL? 50 cm (20 in.)
WHAT SPREAD? 30 cm (12 in.)
WHY GROW IT? Great garden dahlia, perfect for pollinators, great for containers

'Ellen Huston'▲

This dwarf decorative dahlia is great for all sorts of container plantings, and for borders and bedding out too. It has bold, intense, fully double orange blooms, sometimes showing their deep orange centres, and good deep black foliage. Plants are compact and floriferous. Winner of a Royal Horticultural Society Award of Garden Merit.

WHAT TYPE? Dwarf decorative
HOW TALL? 70 cm (28 in.)
WHAT SPREAD? 30 cm (12 in.)
WHY GROW IT? Good garden dahlia, great for containers, good bedding dahlia variety, good dark foliage

YELLOW

You can find a huge number of yellow dahlia varieties in a wide range of shades, tints, and tones. A bright, smack-you-right-between-the-eyes acid yellow is quite common, but I find this fierce hue difficult to get on with in the garden. If possible, see yellow varieties first-hand before you buy. Over the years I've ordered a few that I've quickly donated to friends with an allotment once they've come into flower, in the hope that planted safely behind a row of runner beans the high-visibility blooms won't startle too many chickens.

Use yellow dahlia varieties with caution in mixed herbaceous borders. Combining with lots of other bold yellow flowers can work, but a careful choice of the more golden or amber varieties is still necessary. Sometimes only the late-summer North American prairie daisies like asters, rudbeckias, heleniums, helianthus, and coreopsis can stand up to yellow dahlias. However, if you love the powerful, strong, sharp yellows, go for those with deep bronze or black foliage, which have the most impact. I prefer the rich golden, almost yolky, varieties, or the amber, apricot, and peachy yellow cultivars that nearly sink into pale orange. The very pale and creamy primrose yellows are also well worth planting.

'Bishop of York'◂

Truly golden yellow is a surprisingly rare colour in dahlias, but this wonderful single with fabulous dark bronze foliage is probably as close as it gets. The soft golden to bronze yellow blooms work brilliantly against the dark leaves and, like the other Bishops, this one grows well in containers and in all sorts of garden situations.

WHAT TYPE? Single
HOW TALL? 75 cm (30 in.)
WHAT SPREAD? 61 cm (24 in.)
WHY GROW IT? Great garden variety, great container dahlia, perfect for pollinators

'Appleblossom'▴

A delicate apricot yellow collerette variety that has pale creamy yellow petals with a very pale rose pink collar. Long stems, perfect for cutting, and a great garden dahlia for beds and borders.

WHAT TYPE? Collerette
HOW TALL? 75 cm (30 in.)
WHAT SPREAD? 61 cm (24 in.)
WHY GROW IT? Great garden variety, great for containers, perfect for pollinators

'Lucky Ducky'▸

The outer petals of anemone 'Lucky Ducky' are the softest pale yellow, but the central pincushion is much deeper—an exploding egg yolk of tiny yellow florets. I've become rather fond of it and discovered it looks marvellous planted among *Anthemis* 'Sauce Hollandaise'. A similar variety is 'Lemon Puff', which has equally good, bright yellow flowers on a slightly shorter, less upright plant (see page 46).

WHAT TYPE? Anemone
HOW TALL? 122 cm (48 in.)
WHAT SPREAD? 61 cm (24 in.)
WHY GROW THEM? Great garden variety, good for cutting, great container dahlia

'Knockout'◂

SYNONYM 'Mystic Illusion'

While it might have slightly too much full-on fierce yellow for some, this single variety certainly lives up to its name. It has shockingly vibrant blooms on a dwarf plant that requires little to no staking, and the most amazing dark black ferny leaves. This variety overflows with youthful yellow dahlia exuberance. Winner of a Royal Horticultural Society Award of Garden Merit.

WHAT TYPE? Single
HOW TALL? 75 cm (30 in.)
WHAT SPREAD? 61 cm (24 in.)
WHY GROW IT? Great garden variety, great for containers, perfect for pollinators

'Happy Single Party'▾

Two single varieties in a very similar vein to 'Knockout'. Both have a similar contrast of shocking canary yellow blooms and dark bronze to black foliage, and well worth growing. Great for containers. 'Yellow Hammer'◂ is winner of a Royal Horticultural Society Award of Garden Merit.

WHAT TYPE? Single
HOW TALL? 76–100 cm (30–40 in.)
WHAT SPREAD? 50–61 cm (20–24 in.)
WHY GROW THEM? Great garden varieties, great for containers, perfect for pollinators, great for bedding displays

'Verrone's Taylor Swift'

This new, very unusual variety is a golden flame–petalled stellar dahlia with rich yellow petals that on the reverse look like they've been licked by orange-red flames. Right at the edge of the petals are the finest thin red markings that perfectly highlight the form of the bloom. Good strong plant and long stems. Fiery perfection.

WHAT TYPE? Stellar
HOW TALL? 100 cm (40 in.)
WHAT SPREAD? 50 cm (20 in.)
WHY GROW IT? Great garden variety, good cut flower

'Yellow Bird'

A double yellow collerette with a golden central disc. I rather love the slightly fluffy, feathery, pale yellow collar petals. It's almost blowsy for a collerette, and the blooms are a good 10 cm (4 in.) across. Quite large and slightly pointed outer petals add to the show. It makes relatively small tubers, so it's a good choice for creating pot tubers to ensure you can overwinter successfully.

WHAT TYPE? Collerette
HOW TALL? 120 cm (47 in.)
WHAT SPREAD? 77 cm (30 in.)
WHY GROW IT? Great garden variety, great cut flower, perfect for pollinators

'Impression Fortuna'

One of the Impression series of dwarf collerette dahlias, this variety is a rich yolky yellow that's great for all sorts of containers. Charming and cheery, with good green foliage. The blooms are held high above the foliage on clean stems.

WHAT TYPE? Collerette
HOW TALL? 50 cm (20 in.)
WHAT SPREAD? 30 cm (12 in.)
WHY GROW IT? Great garden variety, great for containers, perfect for pollinators, great for bedding displays

'Clair de Lune'▸

A fresh lemon yellow collerette of impeccable form with a very slightly lighter creamy yellow collar and a deep golden yellow central disc. Looks great when grown with lots of perennial *Anthemis* daisies and also with purple *Verbena bonariensis*. Winner of a Royal Horticultural Society Award of Garden Merit.

WHAT TYPE? Collerette
HOW TALL? 100 cm (40 in.)
WHAT SPREAD? 50 cm (20 in.)
WHY GROW IT? Great garden variety, perfect for pollinators, great cut flower

'Chic'▾

This delightful little dark-leaved dahlia is perfect for pots and containers. It's a pretty peony type with a lovely mellow buttery yellow colour. Short and compact, with rusty golden eyes at the centre of the blooms.

WHAT TYPE? Peony/semi-double
HOW TALL? 40 cm (16 in.)
WHAT SPREAD? 40 cm (16 in.)
WHY GROW IT? Great garden variety, great for containers, perfect for pollinators

'Yellow Star'

Quite a large-flowered pale yellow cactus dahlia that retains its rich buttery yellow colour at the centre of the bloom fading toward the tips of the petals. If you catch it up close, in the right light, it's stunning. A magical yellow variety.

WHAT TYPE? Cactus
HOW TALL? 120 cm (47 in.)
WHAT SPREAD? 60 cm (24 in.)
WHY GROW IT? Great tall border variety, great cut flower

'Gramma's Lemon Pie'▲

I'm not normally a fan of dahlias that have coloured petals with a distinct area of white toward the tip, which can lend an old-fashioned feel to the bloom. However, this variety is an exception. The colour of the petal is a lovely pale lemony apricot and it works beautifully. It's like vintage lemon meringue dahlia pie.

WHAT TYPE? Formal decorative
HOW TALL? 120 cm (47 in.)
WHAT SPREAD? 60 cm (24 in.)
WHY GROW IT? Great tall border variety, great cut flower

'Ginger Snap'▲

This is a gorgeous little golden waterlily dahlia with small glowing blooms on strong sturdy stems that make great cut flowers. It's a good compact plant for the garden, and the flowers are a rich gingery gold, fading to caramel yellow.

WHAT TYPE? Waterlily
HOW TALL? 90 cm (36 in.)
WHAT SPREAD? 40 cm (16 in.)
WHY GROW IT? Great cut flower, great garden dahlia, good for containers

'Nippon'▸

I love this teeny-weeny dwarf yellow dahlia. Tiny buttermilk yellow blooms with chocolate centres sit above dark bronze ferny foliage. It's very small dahlia, bright as a button, and perfect for containers and window boxes.

WHAT TYPE? Single
HOW TALL? 40 cm (16 in.)
WHAT SPREAD? 30 cm (12 in.)
WHY GROW IT? Great for containers, good dark foliage, perfect for pollinators, floriferous, great for bedding displays

'Ryecroft Marge'

This dahlia definitely appeals to my mischievous side. It's a canary yellow and pale pink powder puff of pure fun. It's bound to raise more than a few eyebrows among the good-taste brigade, but anemone dahlias are rather adept at doing that anyway. If Marge Simpson had a favourite dahlia, I do hope it would be this one. Winner of a Royal Horticultural Society Award of Garden Merit.

WHAT TYPE? Anemone
HOW TALL? 120 cm (47 in.)
WHAT SPREAD? 60 cm (24 in.)
WHY GROW IT? Great tall border variety, great cut flower, unusual colour combination

CORAL PINK AND SUNSET

There are so many good coral dahlia varieties that I think they deserve their very own section. My definition of *coral* includes dahlias that are a simple pink-orange blend or have complex combinations of yellows, oranges, reds, and pinks within the bloom. I also include those that exhibit strong splashes of the colours of a dramatic summer sunset as their blooms develop and mature. Deep pink and orange are two of my favourite colours, so these dahlias provide me with a very good deal indeed. The deliciously varied and rich tones in these blooms treat my eyes to a sugary summer feast. Fans of Tequila Sunrise cocktails and tropical sunsets may grow rather fond of these dahlias.

'Waltzing Mathilda'

A great garden variety with unusual informal peach-coral peony blooms, sometimes with a cherry red blush. Dark burgundy-black foliage sets them off brilliantly. Great in the border or in containers. A whirling dahlia dervish.

WHAT TYPE? Peony
HOW TALL? 60 cm (24 in.)
WHAT SPREAD? 40 cm (16 in.)
WHY GROW IT? Great garden dahlia, perfect for pollinators, great for containers

'Twyning's Revel'

I'm a huge fan of so many of dahlia breeder Mark Twyning's offerings, but this is my favourite. Absolutely stunning deep pink to orange-pink single to almost peony form blooms with golden yellow halos surrounding a dark chocolate central disc. It has gorgeous black foliage too. Revel in its sunset colours.

WHAT TYPE? Single
HOW TALL? 60 cm (24 in.)
WHAT SPREAD? 30 cm (12 in.)
WHY GROW IT? Great garden dahlia, perfect for pollinators, great for containers

'Falcon's Future'

A hot pink-and-yellow coral explosion. I love the drama of this medium to large semi-cactus. Just one bloom in a vase is a complete knockout. It's a mad mix of golden yellow, coral, and cerise pink. Fabulous, but not for the faint of heart.

WHAT TYPE? Semi-cactus
HOW TALL? 100 cm (40 in.)
WHAT SPREAD? 50 cm (20 in.)
WHY GROW IT? Total diva, great cut flower

'Shea's Rainbow'

With this variety I'm taking a step out of my usual colour comfort zone into variegated dahlias, but I absolutely love it. Flecks of cherry pink, cerise, and red fly among coral pink-yellow cactus petals on a medium-size bloom. It's gaudy gorgeousness.

WHAT TYPE? Cactus
HOW TALL? 122 cm (48 in.)
WHAT SPREAD? 60 cm (24 in.)
WHY GROW IT? Total diva, great cut flower

'Satellite'

A tall, strong, hot pink semi-cactus with petals that blend into yellow right at their base. Substantial blooms around 20 cm (8 in.) in diameter. Fuchsia pink flamboyance.

WHAT TYPE? Semi-cactus
HOW TALL? 122 cm (48 in.)
WHAT SPREAD? 60 cm (24 in.)
WHY GROW IT? Total diva, great cut flower, good tall herbaceous border variety

'Giggles' ▼

These are two perky little collerettes. 'Giggles' has dusty coral-orange petals and a paler rosy pink collar around a bright gold centre, and 'Pipsqueak' ▶ sports a more rose-watermelon and candy-coral pink combination. Both are lively colour combinations and look great among orange crocosmias and chocolate foliage in the herbaceous border. They flower profusely too. Great for small gardens.

WHAT TYPE? Collerette
HOW TALL? 106 cm (42 in.)
WHAT SPREAD? 50 cm (20 in.)
WHY GROW THEM? Great garden dahlias, perfect for pollinators, great cut flower dahlias, good for containers and borders

'Wannabee'

This is almost an anemone dahlia, but its form can be variable! It's an amazing fusion of colours, with gold, flame, and tangerine orange at the centre blending out into deep pinks that are almost mauve. The tubular petals at the centre of the bloom appear slightly crimped, or fimbriated, and as the flowers mature, they add extra fizz to proceedings. They will spice up your life.

WHAT TYPE? Unclassified/anemone
HOW TALL? 122 cm (48 in.)
WHAT SPREAD? 60 cm (24 in.)
WHY GROW IT? Great garden dahlia, great cut flower, unusual colour combination

'Fire Magic'

One of my most sumptuous fuchsia and coral-pink dahlias. It's totally magical, and I can't live without it. It's hard to capture all the incredible colours mixed up in the petals, which include fuchsia pink, orange, cherry, and watermelon red. The blooms are about 15 cm (6 in.) across and on quite long straight stems. Fiery fabulousness.

WHAT TYPE? Semi-cactus
HOW TALL? 137 cm (54 in.)
WHAT SPREAD? 60 cm (24 in.)
WHY GROW IT? Good tall herbaceous border dahlia, great cut flower dahlia, total diva, unusual colour

‘Yelno Enchantment’▲

Delightful shades of pink blend together on the golden yellow petals of this small flowered waterlily variety. The central nose of the bloom appears almost lavender-pink, as the unfurling petals are slightly purple on their reverse side. Good strong stems for cutting.

WHAT TYPE? Waterlily
HOW TALL? 100 cm (40 in.)
WHAT SPREAD? 40 cm (16 in.)
WHY GROW IT? Great cut flower, good garden variety, unusual colour combination

‘Foxy Lady’▸

An unusual antique rose, coral pink, and creamy yellow formal decorative dahlia with a deeper rose, almost mauve, reverse to its petals. Good cut-flower variety with strong stems on a robust plant.

WHAT TYPE? Formal decorative
HOW TALL? 122 cm (48 in.)
WHAT SPREAD? 56 cm (22 in.)
WHY GROW IT? Total diva, great cut flower, good garden variety

'Jitterbug'

A bright pink decorative, almost waterlily variety that's a great garden dahlia. Quite an unusual salmon pink blends to bright yellow at the base of the broad petals. It comes into flower early and goes on well into the autumn months.

WHAT TYPE? Decorative
HOW TALL? 90 cm (36 in.)
WHAT SPREAD? 50 cm (20 in.)
WHY GROW IT? Great cut flower, good garden variety, early and prolific bloomer, compact variety

'Sonic Bloom'

A fabulous coral pink fizz. This informal decorative dahlia is full of fluffy petals that are a blend of pink and mauve with a tiny hint of yellow. Attractive dark flower stems also add to the display, as do the double split tips of each individual petal, which give the bloom a ruffled or crimped appearance. Great cut flower, strong green foliage, and capable of causing a scene in any border display.

WHAT TYPE? Informal decorative
HOW TALL? 122 cm (48 in.)
WHAT SPREAD? 60 cm (24 in.)
WHY GROW IT? Great cut flower, total diva, unusual colour, good garden dahlia

'Hollyhill Margarita'

A tall and totally tropical-looking incurved cactus variety. Its swirling, tentacle-like petals are a fabulous exotic blend of hot pink and orange with a hint of yellow at their base. It's quite a big plant with long elegant stems great for cutting, and would look amazing with tall herbaceous late summer perennials. A heady, tantalizing cocktail.

WHAT TYPE? Cactus
HOW TALL? 152 cm (60 in.)
WHAT SPREAD? 70 cm (28 in.)
WHY GROW IT? Great cut flower, total diva, unusual colour, good for tall herbaceous border

'Floorinoor'

An anemone dahlia with all kinds of crazy pink, orange, and yellow colour combinations across the blooms. I love it, and I also like the fact that there can be quite a lot of variation in the form and colours of the blooms on the same plant. It has good dark green-bronze foliage too. A fun and funky flower.

WHAT TYPE? Anemone
HOW TALL? 100 cm (40 in.)
WHAT SPREAD? 50 cm (20 in.)
WHY GROW IT? Great garden dahlia, good green-bronze foliage, good for borders or containers

‘Happy Single Flame’▲

It’s difficult to pick a category for these two brilliant singles, but both have touches of orange red, pink, and yellow and both bring to mind sunrises and sunsets. ‘Flame’ has rich red-pink petals that bleed into strong yellow toward the centre of the bloom and is a winner of a Royal Horticultural Society Award of Garden Merit. ‘Happy Single First Love’▶ is slightly more subtle, with apricot-pink petals that have a splash of red-orange at their base. Like all the Happy Singles range, these two varieties have glorious dark foliage. I’m particularly fond of this series, which is part of an ever-increasing range of small dahlias perfect for tiny gardens and patio pots.

WHAT TYPE? Single
HOW TALL? 80 cm (32 in.)
WHAT SPREAD? 30 cm (12 in.)
WHY GROW THEM? Great for containers, perfect for pollinators, great for small gardens and patios, good dark foliage

'Karma Fuchsiana'

A stunningly bright fuchsia-pink and coral decorative dahlia. Part of the Karma series of varieties selected for their strong, sturdy stems and long vase life. A brilliant cut flower variety, but a great dahlia for the herbaceous border too.

WHAT TYPE? Decorative
HOW TALL? 80 cm (32 in.)
WHAT SPREAD? 50 cm (20 in.)
WHY GROW IT? Total diva, great cut flower, good garden variety, strong and unusual colour

'Twilite'

Pretty pale pink petals surround a deeper magenta pincushion of florets with golden tips. An unusual floriferous anemone that I can't help but love.

WHAT TYPE? Anemone
HOW TALL? 122 cm (48 in.)
WHAT SPREAD? 50 cm (20 in.)
WHY GROW IT? Great garden dahlia, good cut flower, prolific bloomer

'Karma Sangria'

I could stare into the blooms of sunset dahlias like 'Karma Sangria' for days. It is energizing, colourful, and warm. This variety may be a bit rhubarb and custard for some, but I love it. It's a great garden cactus and a member of the Karma series of sturdy cut-flower varieties.

WHAT TYPE? Cactus
HOW TALL? 110 cm (43 in.)
WHAT SPREAD? 50 cm (20 in.)
WHY GROW IT? Great cut flower, good garden dahlia

'Nenekazi'

'Nenekazi' runs a close contest with 'Shea's Rainbow' as the ultimate sunset variety. This dahlia's petals twist and flick in the most fantastic way. I absolutely adore it. An impressive cut flower and border dahlia.

WHAT TYPE? Fimbriated semi-cactus
HOW TALL? 140 cm (55 in.)
WHAT SPREAD? 65 cm (26 in.)
WHY GROW IT? Great cut flower, good tall garden dahlia, gorgeous sunset diva

PINK

Horticulturally speaking, for me the sentence "Love is . . ." has always been rather easy to complete: "Love is a pink dahlia." With pink dahlias, the combinations of colours that make up a particular tint, tone, or shade can be hugely complex, as so many different colours are involved all under one banner. I'm usually drawn toward the deeper, stronger pinks like magenta, cherry, and raspberry. But I also adore fuchsia, coral, ruby, and cerise. The paler, softer mid and pale pinks like candy, carnation, rose, and dusky antique also have a huge amount to offer in the garden. They work well with other pastel tints, pale tones, and white. All are grouped together in this section. Enjoy your exploration in pink.

'Fascination'

A very bright, slightly purple-pink peony dahlia with rather large, blowsy petals. Combined with the dark burgundy-black foliage it's a fantastic contrast. A solid pink and a great garden variety. Winner of a Royal Horticultural Society Award of Garden Merit.

WHAT TYPE? Peony
HOW TALL? 90 cm (36 in.)
WHAT SPREAD? 50 cm (20 in.)
WHY GROW IT? Great garden dahlia, perfect for pollinators, good for containers

'Jazzy' ▲

Two gorgeous double pink collerette varieties. 'Jazzy' has slightly broader, bigger petals with a bold splash of deep cherry pink that bleeds out to a paler pink at the edges. This works brilliantly, as it amplifies the contrast of the slightly paler pink collar petals. 'Twyning's Pink Fish' ▶ is similar, with slightly smaller blooms and sometimes more than one layer of large petals; it's a winner of a Royal Horticultural Society Award of Garden Merit. Both are great garden dahlias.

WHAT TYPE? Collerette
HOW TALL? 90–120 cm (36–47 in.)
WHAT SPREAD? 50–60 cm (20–24 in.)
WHY GROW IT? Great cut flower, great garden dahlia, perfect for pollinators, good for containers

'Rotonde'

There are so many wonderful pink cactus dahlias to choose from, but this glorious variety has such an open globe shape to its blooms, and the way it holds them on the top of elegant stems is stunning. Relatively small to medium-size blooms for a cactus on a robust plant.

WHAT TYPE? Cactus
HOW TALL? 110 cm (43 in.)
WHAT SPREAD? 50 cm (20 in.)
WHY GROW IT? Great cut flower, great border dahlia

'Bonne Espérance'

A dainty little single mignon or lilliput dahlia. You'll find the sweetest candy pink blooms only 2.5 cm (1 in.) across on a short, stocky plant. Jolly and perfect for window boxes, containers, and all sorts of small garden situations. It's a baby-doll dahlia.

WHAT TYPE? Single
HOW TALL? 30 cm (12 in.)
WHAT SPREAD? 20 cm (8 in.)
WHY GROW IT? Perfect for pollinators, perfect for small gardens, great for containers and window boxes, early and prolific bloomer

'Rosy Wings'

This perfectly formed pastel pink collerette has both outer petals and collar petals in an identical mid-pink tone. Neat 8 cm (3 in.) blooms on a smart floriferous plant with good strong stems. Marshmallow pink perfection. 'Jane Horton' is a similar and equally good garden variety (see page 47).

WHAT TYPE? Collerette
HOW TALL? 122 cm (48 in.)
WHAT SPREAD? 50 cm (20 in.)
WHY GROW IT? Perfect for pollinators, great garden dahlia, good cut flower

'Northwest Cosmos'

This is listed as a lilac and purple blend, but to my eye it's more of a mid-pink with a central halo of deepest magenta surrounding a sunny golden yellow disc. It is a good vigorous single variety that, as its name suggests, brings to mind tall pink *Cosmos bipinnatus* hybrids. A great tall border dahlia for the garden. Winner of a Royal Horticultural Society Award of Garden Merit.

WHAT TYPE? Single
HOW TALL? 152 cm (60 in.)
WHAT SPREAD? 60 cm (24 in.)
WHY GROW IT? Great garden dahlia, stunning green foliage, perfect for pollinators

'Jeanne D'Arc'▲

A bright pink giant cactus that's pretty spectacular and great fun to grow. Huge blooms you could lose yourself in. A total diva that wants eyes to pop and jaws to drop. Astonishing.

WHAT TYPE? Cactus
HOW TALL? 100 cm (40 in.)
WHAT SPREAD? 40 cm (16 in.)
WHY GROW IT? Total diva, great cut flower

'Pearl of Heemstede'▼

This classic pale to mid-pink waterlily variety is floriferous with fantastic long stems. It looks amazing floating among *Verbena bonariensis* and giant feather grass. Winner of a Royal Horticultural Society Award of Garden Merit.

WHAT TYPE? Waterlily
HOW TALL? 152 cm (60 in.)
WHAT SPREAD? 75 cm (30 in.)
WHY GROW IT? Great cut flower, great tall border variety, floriferous

'Happy Single Wink' ▸

Two of the Happy Single series of dark-leaved dahlias. 'Wink' is a jolly rich pink with a deep cherry halo around a dark central eye, and is winner of a Royal Horticultural Society Award of Garden Merit. I rather like this cheeky fellow. 'Juliet' ▼ is a simple purple pink single, but also very good. Cheery floriferous varieties for all sorts of containers and situations in the garden.

WHAT TYPE? Single
HOW TALL? 75 cm (30 in.)
WHAT SPREAD? 46 cm (18 in.)
WHY GROW THEM? Great garden varieties, good container varieties, floriferous, perfect for pollinators

'Classic Rosamunde'

One of the Classic series of dark-leaved varieties, 'Rosamunde' is a bright, cheery, perfectly formed pink peony. It has deep purple bronze stems and foliage and is perfect for the border or growing in containers. A smart, compact, and floriferous variety.

WHAT TYPE? Peony
HOW TALL? 100 cm (40 in.)
WHAT SPREAD? 50 cm (20 in.)
WHY GROW IT? Great garden dahlia, perfect for pollinators, compact and floriferous, good dark foliage

'Jill Day'

This small flowered-cactus dahlia is an unusual shade of dusky rose-pink. Good dark green foliage and crimson stems. It's rather special.

WHAT TYPE? Cactus
HOW TALL? 120 cm (47 in.)
WHAT SPREAD? 50 cm (20 in.)
WHY GROW IT? Great cut flower, good tall border dahlia, unusual colour

'Candy Eyes'

SYNONYM 'Mystic Dreamer'

A pink-and-white-striped single dahlia with jet black foliage. Perfect for pots and growing in all sorts of containers as well as in the border. Looks great with silver-leaved foliage plants.

WHAT TYPE? Single
HOW TALL? 75 cm (30 in.)
WHAT SPREAD? 50 cm (20 in.)
WHY GROW IT? Great for containers, perfect for pollinators, compact and floriferous, great dark foliage

'Sweetheart'◂

SYNONYM 'Freya's Sweetheart'

A hot-pink-and-white bicoloured dwarf single that is very aptly named. It's a very jolly, perky dahlia and compact, with good green foliage. This cheerful poppet is perfect for small pots and window boxes.

WHAT TYPE? Single
HOW TALL? 25 cm (10 in.)
WHAT SPREAD? 20 cm (8 in.)
WHY GROW IT? Great for small containers, perfect for pollinators, compact and floriferous, good green foliage

'Pontiac'◂

'Pontiac' and 'She Devil'▾ are two wonderful, rich, vivid pink cactus dahlia varieties that I love. Both have blooms approximately 10 cm (4 in.) across that are super spiky and have a very slight golden glow that emanates from the base of the petals. Both are quite tall with good dark green foliage.

WHAT TYPE? Cactus
HOW TALL? 152 cm (60 in.)
WHAT SPREAD? 100 cm (40 in.)
WHY GROW IT? Great tall border variety, good dark green foliage, diva

'Pink Giraffe'

A delightful double orchid striped swizzle stick of a dahlia. Love, love, love it! Great in the garden among plants with dark bronze, black, and silver foliage. It's low growing and good in containers too. Winner of a Royal Horticultural Society Award of Garden Merit.

WHAT TYPE? Double orchid
HOW TALL? 60 cm (24 in.)
WHAT SPREAD? 30 cm (12 in.)
WHY GROW IT? Great garden dahlia, good green divided foliage, good for containers, unusual

'Shannon'

An old favourite of mine, 'Shannon' is a purple pink decorative dahlia with small to medium-size blooms. In my garden soil it can take on a slightly coral-pink appearance as the bloom ages, although in bud it is more pink-purple. A good garden dahlia.

WHAT TYPE? Decorative
HOW TALL? 100 cm (40 in.)
WHAT SPREAD? 40 cm (16 in.)
WHY GROW IT? Great garden dahlia, compact plant, lovely crisp form

'Mambo'

A shaggy, fluffy, adorable mauve-pink anemone dahlia. There is a riot of tiny double fimbriated cherry pink petals at its centre, with a lion's main of magenta petals that have a slight purple blush on their reverse. A fabulously colourful character.

WHAT TYPE? Anemone
HOW TALL? 90 cm (36 in.)
WHAT SPREAD? 50 cm (20 in.)
WHY GROW IT? Great cut flower, unusual colour, great garden dahlia

'Hillcrest Royal'

Probably my number-one classic cactus dahlia. Most dahlia growers I know adore it as much as I do. Its almost glowing shade of strong magenta-purple-pink can be more of a raspberry on some soils. It is hard to beat, and a favourite of the late great British dahlia guru Christopher Lloyd. Grow it and you'll see why. Winner of a Royal Horticultural Society Award of Garden Merit.

WHAT TYPE? Cactus
HOW TALL? 120 cm (47 in.)
WHAT SPREAD? 50 cm (20 in.)
WHY GROW IT? Great cut flower, classic garden dahlia, great for borders

'Roxy'

One of the best dwarf single magenta varieties. It has a very deep, dark central eye with good deep black-green foliage. Perfect for pots, and flowers all summer long.

WHAT TYPE? Single
HOW TALL? 50 cm (20 in.)
WHAT SPREAD? 30 cm (12 in.)
WHY GROW IT? Great garden dahlia, great for containers, perfect for pollinators

'Bishop of Canterbury'

Another really good Bishop. This gorgeous one has delicate, ferny, bronze-black foliage and deep cherry-magenta single flowers with dark plum, almost chocolate, centres.

WHAT TYPE? Single
HOW TALL? 110 cm (43 in.)
WHAT SPREAD? 50 cm (20 in.)
WHY GROW IT? Great garden dahlia, good for containers, perfect for pollinators

'Magenta Star'

Magenta magnifica. If ever a dahlia had the wow factor, it is this sensational pink-purple single. Its starry, deep magenta blooms glow above finely divided gunmetal black foliage. This towering variety looks amazing among lofty perennials in a mixed herbaceous border. Winner of a Royal Horticultural Society Award of Garden Merit.

WHAT TYPE? Single
HOW TALL? 152 cm (60 in.)
WHAT SPREAD? 60 cm (24 in.)
WHY GROW IT? Great garden dahlia, perfect for pollinators, stunning foliage, great tall border dahlia, unusual colour

'Ooh La La'▲

A sumptuous, heavy-blooming informal decorative dahlia with deep pink to lavender-pink blooms. The petals are split ever so slightly at the tips, which gives the bloom a more relaxed, slightly frou-frou appearance. Floral French fancy.

WHAT TYPE? Informal decorative
HOW TALL? 122 cm (48 in.)
WHAT SPREAD? 60 cm (24 in.)
WHY GROW IT? Great garden dahlia, great cut flower, diva

'Englehardt's Matador'▲

This variety has the attitude of a big, tall, blowsy, dinner-plate dahlia, but on a short, stocky plant. Shockingly gorgeous hot pink 15 cm (6 in.) decorative blooms on a compact variety. It also has good dark purple-green foliage and grows well in a container. Looks amazing planted among silver foliage.

WHAT TYPE? Decorative
HOW TALL? 90 cm (36 in.)
WHAT SPREAD? 30 cm (12 in.)
WHY GROW IT? Great garden dahlia, good for containers, diva, heavy bloomer

'Teesbrooke Redeye' ▸

Very pretty lavender-pink collerette with a dark bronze centre. Good foliage and a very handsome-looking plant. Nice long stems for cutting, and the bees and butterflies go mad for it.

WHAT TYPE? Collerette
HOW TALL? 90 cm (36 in.)
WHAT SPREAD? 40 cm (16 in.)
WHY GROW IT? Great garden dahlia, good for containers, perfect for pollinators

'Fairway Pilot' ◂

A rich, hot pink, giant informal decorative dahlia that has the most wonderful wavy petals. It is meant for deep, herbaceous borders. If you have room, it's well worth growing this delicious diva.

WHAT TYPE? Informal decorative
HOW TALL? 160 cm (63 in.)
WHAT SPREAD? 70 cm (28 in.)
WHY GROW IT? Total diva, great for tall herbaceous borders, strong colour, great cut flower

PURPLE, LILAC, AND LAVENDER

There are no truly blue dahlias, but you can find a surprising number of purple varieties that are a very deep regal shade with distinctly more in common with blue than red or pink. They have a velvety, princely presence and look wonderful with tall golden yellow perennial daisies like helianthus, helianthemums, and rudbeckias, and strong tangerine orange flowers such as the Mexican sunflower and lion's tail.

There are also lots of lavender and lilac varieties that look great in the garden and work well with other pastel tints and tones. Many of my favourite purple dahlia varieties are actually blends and bicolour mixes of purple with lilac, lavender, cream, and white, some of which are included in this section.

'Thomas A. Edison'◂

This truly deep purple medium- to large-flowered decorative dahlia puts on quite a show. It looks amazing with other richly coloured dahlias, particularly bright red, tangerine orange, and magenta ones. Also stunning among big, statuesque grasses in a tall, mixed herbaceous border setting.

WHAT TYPE? Decorative
HOW TALL? 120 cm (47 in.)
WHAT SPREAD? 60 cm (24 in.)
WHY GROW IT? Good tall herbaceous border variety, great cut flower, rich and deep colour

'Moor Place'◂

A very deep plum pompon. A classic variety and, like any good pom, totally adorable. It has good dark stems and is a great cut-flower dahlia.

WHAT TYPE? Pompon
HOW TALL? 90 cm (36 in.)
WHAT SPREAD? 50 cm (20 in.)
WHY GROW IT? Great cut flower, classic pompon

'Blue Beard'▸

A rich and sumptuous small flowered semi-cactus. Good, strong, elegant stems on quite a tall plant. One of the most blue-purple dahlias I've ever seen.

WHAT TYPE? Semi-cactus
HOW TALL? 120 cm (47 in.)
WHAT SPREAD? 60 cm (24 in.)
WHY GROW IT? Good tall herbaceous border variety, great cut flower, unusual deep colour

'Ambition'▲

A very bright violet semi-cactus dahlia with especially spiky blooms. Brilliant cut flower and good border variety.

WHAT TYPE? Semi-cactus
HOW TALL? 100 cm (40 in.)
WHAT SPREAD? 50 cm (20 in.)
WHY GROW IT? Good herbaceous border variety, great cut flower

'Blue Bayou'▸

An unusual contrasting deep and pale purple anemone. The intensely rich purple central florets are surrounded by large, delicate lilac-coloured petals. Large blooms sit atop dark stems on quite a tall leafy plant. Extraordinary loveliness.

WHAT TYPE? Anemone
HOW TALL? 100 cm (40 in.)
WHAT SPREAD? 50 cm (20 in.)
WHY GROW IT? Good herbaceous border variety, great cut flower, very unusual colour

'Brantwood'▲

'Brantwood' is a smashingly good deep purple single variety. Good green foliage and a prolific bloomer. Bees go bonkers for it.

WHAT TYPE? Single
HOW TALL? 152 cm (60 in.)
WHAT SPREAD? 60 cm (24 in.)
WHY GROW IT? Great garden dahlia, perfect for pollinators, great tall border dahlia

'Downham Royal'▶

This miniature plum red–purple ball is not quite a pompon, but a smart little dahlia you're bound to love. It's dahlia cut-flower perfection.

WHAT TYPE? Ball
HOW TALL? 110 cm (43 in.)
WHAT SPREAD? 60 cm (24 in.)
WHY GROW IT? Great cut flower, strong colour, good form

'The Phantom'

The anemone blooms of this variety can be somewhat variable, but it is a beguiling dahlia. It has a powerful combination of the darkest and deepest plum magenta with a hint of burnt orange to the pincushion centre. It is surrounded by deep pink outer petals with broad splashes of cerise. Set against other rich but bright colours in the border, it is breathtaking and menacingly marvellous.

WHAT TYPE? Anemone
HOW TALL? 100 cm (40 in.)
WHAT SPREAD? 40 cm (16 in.)
WHY GROW IT? Great garden dahlia, good for containers, unusual colour combination

'Boogie Nites'

This powerfully purple delight is a floriferous and strong well-proportioned plant with regal princely appeal. It's a striking variety and a brilliant cut flower.

WHAT TYPE? Formal decorative
HOW TALL? 137 cm (54 in.)
WHAT SPREAD? 60 cm (24 in.)
WHY GROW IT? Good herbaceous border variety, great cut flower

'Lauren Michele'

This is a pale lilac waterlily with a dark purple reverse to the petals. Very floriferous and a great container and border variety. Good compact growing habit.

WHAT TYPE? Waterlily
HOW TALL? 132 cm (52 in.)
WHAT SPREAD? 60 cm (24 in.)
WHY GROW IT? Great for containers, good garden variety, unusual form

'Gonzo Grape'

Another plum purple decorative variety that's strong, robust, and floriferous. It's great for the garden and has fabulous long stems for cutting.

WHAT TYPE? Decorative
HOW TALL? 122 cm (48 in.)
WHAT SPREAD? 60 cm (24 in.)
WHY GROW IT? Great cut flower, good garden variety

'Blackberry Ice'

I love this purple-and-white decorative dahlia. It's a really eye-catching variety and very floriferous. The blooms are a white and pale lilac-lavender blend, with deep splashes of blackberry at the base of the petals that give the blooms a rich purple heart. It has strong, dark, long stems for cutting and good dark green foliage.

WHAT TYPE? Decorative
HOW TALL? 122 cm (48 in.)
WHAT SPREAD? 60 cm (24 in.)
WHY GROW IT? Great cut flower, good garden variety, unusual colour combination

'Lisa Lisa'◂

A delicate, delicious, and gentle lilac-and-white waterlily. The blooms are about 10 cm (4 in.) across on a compact plant with solid green foliage. A good pastel pink-purple variety for all sorts of garden situations.

WHAT TYPE? Waterlily
HOW TALL? 110 cm (43 in.)
WHAT SPREAD? 60 cm (24 in.)
WHY GROW IT? Great garden dahlia, great cut flower, great for containers

'Hugs and Kisses'▸

This is a smart and compact decorative dahlia. The lilac-lavender petals are rolled slightly, giving it the appearance of a stellar dahlia, and the petals have a deep purple reverse. The individual blooms are about 8 cm (3 in.) across. A good garden dahlia that's great for cutting too.

WHAT TYPE? Formal decorative
HOW TALL? 100 cm (40 in.)
WHAT SPREAD? 60 cm (24 in.)
WHY GROW IT? Good garden dahlia, good for cutting, good for containers

'Ivanetti'

This very deep plum purple miniature ball dahlia is a great cut-flower variety. Its intense hue looks amazing in arrangements with other rich, deep-coloured cultivars. Good border dahlia too.

WHAT TYPE? Ball
HOW TALL? 107 cm (42 in.)
WHAT SPREAD? 60 cm (24 in.)
WHY GROW IT? Great cut flower, good garden variety, unusual colour

'Purple Haze'

An incredibly dark, rich, peculiarly pretty purple variety with dark green foliage. The flower form is variable in that some blooms have elements reminiscent of an anemone dahlia, while others are sometimes closer to a peony dahlia. Whatever the form of the blooms, plant this variety among strong, bright, hot colours to help show them off.

WHAT TYPE? Variable (anemone)
HOW TALL? 107 cm (42 in.)
WHAT SPREAD? 60 cm (24 in.)
WHY GROW IT? Good garden variety, very unusual colour, good dark green foliage

'Purpinca'◂

A delightfully odd dwarf anemone. Small deep and dainty purple pink blooms on good green foliage. Perfect in containers (I find it slightly lax and prefer it in a pot). It's a sugarplum fairy. 'Purple Puff' is a similar variety, also great in a container.

WHAT TYPE? Anemone
HOW TALL? 40 cm (16 in.)
WHAT SPREAD? 30 cm (12 in.)
WHY GROW IT? Great for containers, perfect for small gardens, unusual colour

'Teesbrooke Audrey'▸

A delicate and dreamy pale-lavender-and-white collerette. Great for cutting and the garden. A good all-around pastel collerette, and the bees and butterflies seem to love it as much as I do.

WHAT TYPE? Collerette
HOW TALL? 100 cm (40 in.)
WHAT SPREAD? 50 cm (20 in.)
WHY GROW IT? Great garden variety, perfect for pollinators, good for cutting

'Lavender Chiffon'

A luscious white-and-lilac bicoloured semi-cactus. It's quite a tall, lofty plant. I love the way the heavy blooms droop and the gorgeously long petals let it all hang out.

WHAT TYPE? Semi-cactus
HOW TALL? 140 cm (55 in.)
WHAT SPREAD? 60 cm (24 in.)
WHY GROW IT? Good for cutting, total diva, unusual colour and form

'Perfect Partner'

A very gentle lilac-and-white single to semi-double dahlia with dark black foliage. Great for containers and all sorts of garden situations. It requires little to no staking, and in containers lives up to its name with silver and black foliage plants and purple and mauve flowers.

WHAT TYPE? Single to semi-double
HOW TALL? 80 cm (32 in.)
WHAT SPREAD? 35 cm (14 in.)
WHY GROW IT? Great for containers, perfect for pollinators, good garden dahlia

WHITE AND CREAM

I find white flowers to be the lightest and brightest blooms, but often the most difficult to combine with other colours. It's taken me a little longer to appreciate white dahlias, but now—as with all the vibrant varieties—I'm hooked. The whites that I grow, however, probably have to work a little bit harder to impress than the pinks, purples, reds, and oranges do. The upside is that I'm pretty sure the varieties I've included will earn their place in your garden too.

I grow my white dahlias exclusively in a small area of garden below my front window, and in large containers around my front door. This is my mini homage to the famous white garden at Sissinghurst Castle in Kent, England. Colour-wise, these white varieties work best on their own or with other contrasting forms of white flowers. Plant lots and lots of black, purple, plum, silver, dark green, and lime foliage plants to add depth and texture. With a good supporting cast of leafy characters, white and cream dahlias can look magical, restful, and somewhat serene.

'Tsuki Yorine Shisha'▲

A white snowstorm of a dahlia. 'Tsuki Yorine Shisha' is a fimbriated cactus, so the already spiky petals are split at the tips often two or three times to create a giant snowflake effect. Plant with contrasting dahlia forms and unusual foliage plants to show it off. 'Angora'◀ and 'Haseley Bridal Wish'▶ are similar varieties, but much bigger plants with even larger blooms.

WHAT TYPE? Cactus
HOW TALL? 100–160 cm (40–63 in.)
WHAT SPREAD? 50–75 cm (20–30 in.)
WHY GROW THEM? Great cut flower varieties, good garden varieties, unusual flower forms

'Classic Swanlake' ▲

Part of the Classic series of peony-type dahlias with dark bronze and purple-black foliage. Brilliant plants for containers and all sorts of garden situations. 'Swanlake' is a cream, almost primrose-coloured, semi-double with a chocolate central disc. Bees and butterflies love this utterly charming and self-supporting variety.

WHAT TYPE? Peony
HOW TALL? 90 cm (36 in.)
WHAT SPREAD? 50 cm (20 in.)
WHY GROW IT? Great container variety, good garden variety, perfect for pollinators

'Bambino'▲

Mignon, *topmix*, and *lilliput* are terms often applied generally to the smallest dahlia varieties, which are frequently used as dwarf bedding plants. I grow a dahlia labelled 'Topmix White'▼ in my containers. It is one of the sweetest, tiniest daisy-flowered dahlias I have ever seen. Another good lilliput white is 'Bambino'. 'Snow White'◀ is similar, but with pointy petals more like a mini star or single orchid dahlia, and 'Omo'▶ is slightly bigger, but still a dwarf variety, and its blooms have wider, pure white petals; it is a winner of a Royal Horticultural Society Award of Garden Merit. All of them are tidy, daisy-white, and wonderful.

WHAT TYPE? Single
HOW TALL? 30–70 cm (12–28 in.)
WHAT SPREAD? 20–40 cm (8–16 in.)
WHY GROW THEM? Perfect patio and balcony dahlias, good bedding varieties, perfect for pollinators, good for containers

'Platinum Blonde'

This floriferous blond bombshell is a sturdy, robust plant that produces ivory anemone blooms. The outer petals of each flower are a pale pure white, with a central pincushion of creamier florets. Antique white powder puffs on an elegant plant. Great for the garden and for containers.

WHAT TYPE? Anemone
HOW TALL? 122 cm (48 in.)
WHAT SPREAD? 50 cm (20 in.)
WHY GROW IT? Great cut flower, good garden variety, good for containers

'Twyning's After Eight' ◀

'Twyning's After Eight' is a stunning single white variety that's hard to beat. Its incredibly dark jet black foliage is breathtaking, and contrasts dramatically with the many simple, single crisp white blooms with warm yellow-orange centres. It's brilliant and rarely requires any staking. It is also a winner of a Royal Horticultural Society Award of Garden Merit. 'Joe Swift' ▲ is a similarly stunning, dark-leaved variety with bigger single white blooms that have dark centres and larger petals with a slight point to their tips.

WHAT TYPE? Single
HOW TALL? 120 cm (47 in.)
WHAT SPREAD? 60 cm (24 in.)
WHY GROW THEM? Good garden varieties, great for containers, perfect for pollinators

'White Star'

A creamy white medium cactus and a really good all-around variety. I saw it at the Royal Horticultural Society Hampton Court Palace Flower Show planted in a huge drift with white snapdragons, cow parsley, and other white umbels such as white lace flower and Bishop's weed. 'White Star' looked stunning among the contrasting flower forms and shades of white. Twinkle, twinkle, creamy star.

WHAT TYPE? Cactus
HOW TALL? 120 cm (47 in.)
WHAT SPREAD? 60 cm (24 in.)
WHY GROW IT? Good garden variety, great cut flower

'Eveline'

A classy white-and-lilac small decorative dahlia. Perfect white blooms kissed with a gentle lilac colour at the centre and toward the edge of the petals. Delightful.

WHAT TYPE? Decorative
HOW TALL? 120 cm (47 in.)
WHAT SPREAD? 60 cm (24 in.)
WHY GROW IT? Good garden variety, great cut flower, stunning form

'Ice Queen'▲

'Ice Queen' is quite an unusual, relaxed, small white-flowered waterlily. I love the hint of fresh green at the base of its petals. It makes a good strong border plant, with lots and lots of bird-like blooms to create a flighty white flock. I also love 'Le Castel' ▶, a similar pure-white variety and winner of a Royal Horticultural Society Award of Garden Merit.

WHAT TYPE? Waterlily
HOW TALL? 152 cm (60 in.)
WHAT SPREAD? 60 cm (24 in.)
WHY GROW THEM? Good tall border varieties, great cut flowers, pure white

'Bridal Bouquet'▸

'Bridal Bouquet' and 'Cherubino' ▾ are stunning, purely elegant double white collerette varieties. It's hard to choose between them, as they are close to perfection and have good-size blooms roughly 10 cm (4 in.) across. Golden centres are surrounded by a ruffle of white tiny petals and then pure white larger outer petals. These make brilliant border dahlias and are hugely popular with all sorts of pollinating insects.

WHAT TYPE? Collerette
HOW TALL? 120 cm (47 in.)
WHAT SPREAD? 60 cm (24 in.)
WHY GROW THEM? Good garden varieties, great cut flowers, perfect for pollinators

‘Little Snowdrop’

A perfect white pompon variety of gorgeous globular blooms on good straight stems. Adorable, great cut flowers, good border variety. ‘Tiny Treasure’ is another perfect white pompon (see page 50).

WHAT TYPE? Pompon
HOW TALL? 127 cm (50 in.)
WHAT SPREAD? 60 cm (24 in.)
WHY GROW THEM? Good border varieties, great cut flowers

'Star Child'▲

Three sparkly white star or single orchid dahlia varieties. 'White Honka'▼ and 'Tahoma Hope'▶ are the slightly taller varieties with larger blooms, while 'Star Child' is slightly smaller and more compact, with blooms around 8 cm (3 in.) across. All are great in containers and in the border, with strong, straight stems for cutting.

WHAT TYPE? Star or single orchid
HOW TALL? 120 cm (47 in.)
WHAT SPREAD? 60 cm (24 in.)
WHY GROW THEM? Good garden varieties, great cut flowers, perfect for pollinators

'Sterling Silver'

This big, beautiful, bridal white dahlia is a quite large formal decorative type with silky white petals that curve back toward the stem. It has very full and elegant blooms with lush, partially divided dark green foliage, and the stems are tall and strong. It can be a little late to come into bloom, but well worth the wait for the silver satin chic.

WHAT TYPE? Formal decorative
HOW TALL? 152 cm (60 in.)
WHAT SPREAD? 60 cm (24 in.)
WHY GROW IT? Good tall garden variety, great cut flower, large blooms

'Keith's Pet'

A dwarf slightly creamy white single dahlia with flecks of gold at the base of its petals and bronze stems and foliage. A very cheery dahlia for containers. Winner of a Royal Horticultural Society Award of Garden Merit.

WHAT TYPE? Dwarf single
HOW TALL? 52 cm (21 in.)
WHAT SPREAD? 30 cm (12 in.)
WHY GROW IT? Good garden variety, perfect for patios and balconies, good for containers, perfect for pollinators

'Bride To Be'

Along with 'Sterling Silver', another perfect, pure white wedding dahlia. This strong, compact bloom is a classic medium-size waterlily. A pristine variety for cutting and using in floristry.

WHAT TYPE? Waterlily
HOW TALL? 52 cm (21 in.)
WHAT SPREAD? 30 cm (12 in.)
WHY GROW IT? Good garden variety, great cut flower, good form

'Marlene Joy'

A sparkling bright-pink-and-white medium flowered fimbriated semi-cactus. Magically white and wispy petals are touched with cotton candy pink at the tips. When the light hits the blooms they shimmer, and it's joyous and bedazzling to behold.

WHAT TYPE? Fimbriated semi-cactus
HOW TALL? 152 cm (60 in.)
WHAT SPREAD? 60 cm (24 in.)
WHY GROW IT? Great tall border dahlia, great cut flower

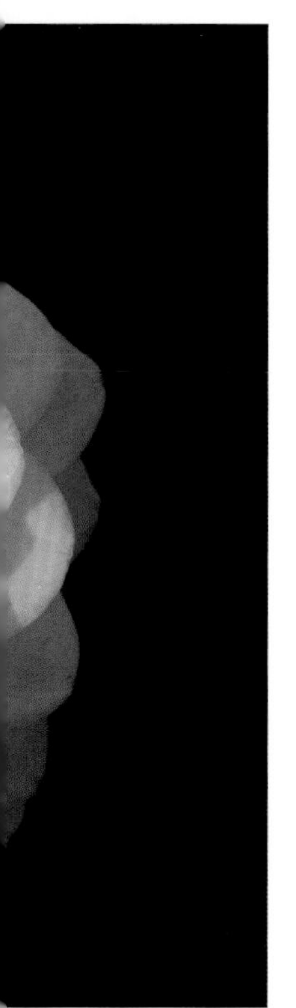

'Happy Days Cream'

This is one of the brilliant Happy Days series of short, dark-leaved dahlias that are perfect for containers. They are available in numerous colours, but my favourite is this creamy white. All of them are very jolly singles with contrasting dark centres. These are compact, basal-branching plants that never seem to stop flowering all season. The Happy Singles range is also excellent, with slightly bigger, taller plants that are still compact and perfect for containers and small gardens. 'Princess' is stunning (see page 44).

WHAT TYPE? Single
HOW TALL? 55–75 cm (22–30 in.)
WHAT SPREAD? 55–65 cm (22–26 in.)
WHY GROW THEM? Great for containers, perfect for pollinators, good dark foliage, floriferous

'Gallery Art Fair'

One of the Gallery series of short container dahlias, which is a good range containing some unusual colour combinations, but this fresh white variety is my favourite. The decorative flower form is almost like a cross between a stellar and waterlily dahlia, and the centre of the bloom has a touch of lime green. Blooms are about 13 cm (5 in.) across. Rather lovely and brilliant for window boxes and balconies. Winner of a Royal Horticultural Society Award of Garden Merit.

WHAT TYPE? Decorative
HOW TALL? 30 cm (12 in.)
WHAT SPREAD? 40 cm (16 in.)
WHY GROW IT? Perfect for containers, great flower form, good green foliage

EXTRATERRESTRIALS

Nice try, tulips. Good effort, roses. However, no one does crazy colour combinations and flower forms quite like dahlias. This final grouping is rather extraordinary and delightfully eccentric, and it contains flowers you'll either love or hate. Some look like they belong on the set of an original episode of *Star Trek*, guest-starring as a super vivid alien flora inhabiting the mysterious Planet Dahlia. To me, they represent the outer limits and extreme vibrancy of dahlias, and they celebrate dahlias' genetic diversity and floral kookiness. These are the varieties that have the pompous horticultural taste police running for the hills. Strange, bizarre, gaudy, weird—whatever you want to call them, I doubt they care. Let's enjoy the dahlias that almost defy categorization. I adore and applaud their fantastic peculiarity.

'Bumble Rumble'

A colourful collerette with raspberry ripple outer petals and an oversize creamy white collar. On the reverse of the outer petals the raspberry pink flourish continues. The long fluffy collar petals almost reach to the end of the outer ones, and there's a large golden mound of florets at the centre. It all lends a clown-like feel to the bloom. Brilliant fun for the garden.

WHAT TYPE? Collerette
HOW TALL? 107 cm (42 in.)
WHAT SPREAD? 30 cm (12 in.)
WHY GROW IT? Great garden dahlia, good for containers, perfect for pollinators, great cut flower, fun flower form

'Fille du Diable'

This is a variegated fiery orange and yellow large semi-cactus. The name translates to "daughter of the devil"! I rather like it, but few orange dahlias can do any wrong in my eyes.

WHAT TYPE? Semi-cactus
HOW TALL? 152 cm (60 in.)
WHAT SPREAD? 70 cm (28 in.)
WHY GROW IT? Great tall border variety, great cut flower, variegated diva

'Twyning's Smartie'

This variety, with random cherry magenta and white petals on a perky single dahlia, has a sweet-shop feel. Sometimes it sports blooms with all-white or all-magenta petals, but usually there is a random number of each. Jolly and a great garden variety.

WHAT TYPE? Single
HOW TALL? 152 cm (60 in.)
WHAT SPREAD? 60 cm (24 in.)
WHY GROW IT? Great garden variety, perfect for pollinators, good for containers

'Boogie Woogie'

This giant canary yellow pincushion centre with a skirt of raspberry ripple pink-and-white petals is certainly not for everyone. The pink also appears on the tips of the central yellow florets as the blooms mature, which adds further mayhem. The central poof almost engulfs the whole anemone bloom as it ages. Don't blame it on the sunshine; blame it on the boogie.

WHAT TYPE? Anemone
HOW TALL? 152 cm (60 in.)
WHAT SPREAD? 60 cm (24 in.)
WHY GROW IT? Great garden variety, kooky colour combination, extraordinary form

'Piperoo'

Variegated blooms can be an acquired taste, just like variegated foliage plants, but I've grown to love their wild and uninhibited glamour. 'Piperoo' is a very stripy, deep cherry-pink-and-white spiky cactus with medium-size blooms on long stems. It's fabulous floral non-conformity.

WHAT TYPE? Cactus
HOW TALL? 140 cm (55 in.)
WHAT SPREAD? 70 cm (28 in.)
WHY GROW IT? Diva, kooky colour combination, great cut flower

'Junkyard Dog'

This super bright, big-bloomed single variety has day-glo cherry pink flowers with white streaking to the petals. A yellow splash at the base of each petal creates a golden sunburst effect. As if that wasn't enough, in the centre is a rich fuzzy orange boss of stamens. A strong, upright, and floriferous variety that blooms late but produces enormous flowers around 18 cm (7 in.) in diameter. *Dazzling* could be an understatement.

WHAT TYPE? Single
HOW TALL? 152 cm (60 in.)
WHAT SPREAD? 60 cm (24 in.)
WHY GROW IT? Great garden variety, perfect for pollinators, huge single blooms

'Fuzzy Wuzzy'

I'm strangely drawn to the vintage feel of this strong, robust variety. It brings to mind pink gingham tablecloths, spotty teapots, and brightly iced cupcakes. It's a medium-size informal decorative dahlia with crimped petal tips that create a unique fuzziness. The petals are a rich candy pink, some tipped with bright white, and it has glossy green foliage.

WHAT TYPE? Informal decorative
HOW TALL? 122 cm (48 in.)
WHAT SPREAD? 60 cm (24 in.)
WHY GROW IT? Great garden variety, good cut flower, vintage dahlia feel

'Pooh' ▲

A popular collerette variety with great form and a strong contrast between the deep tangerine orange petals and bright yellow collar. Blooms are about 10 cm (4 in.) across and sometimes have a splash of yellow at the tips of the petals. Great collerette dahlia for the garden and a very prolific bloomer. Winner of a Royal Horticultural Society Award of Garden Merit.

WHAT TYPE? Collerette
HOW TALL? 152 cm (60 in.)
WHAT SPREAD? 60 cm (24 in.)
WHY GROW IT? Great garden variety, good cut flower, perfect for pollinators, great form

'Hollyhill Spiderwoman' ▶

A truly extraterrestrial spiky cactus. Darkest plum magenta quill-like petals with a white reverse and white tips swirl inside a very exotic-looking bloom. Petals can also appear flushed with golden yellow at the base. A big plant but a very exciting dahlia to grow. Incredible.

WHAT TYPE? Cactus
HOW TALL? 182 cm (72 in.)
WHAT SPREAD? 60 cm (24 in.)
WHY GROW IT? Great tall border variety, good cut flower, unusual colour and form, total diva

'Gitty Up'

A rich orange and rusty red anemone with deep dark green foliage. The central pincushion of florets is a deep bronze, while the outer petals are pale orange licked with streaks of red that fade toward the tips. Good dark bronze stems too.

WHAT TYPE? Anemone
HOW TALL? 107 cm (42 in.)
WHAT SPREAD? 40 cm (16 in.)
WHY GROW IT? Great garden variety, kooky colour combination, great darkest-green foliage

'Poodle Skirt'

Another curious anemone dahlia that I can't help but love. Magenta and berry colours combine in the pincushion poof of the centre of the bloom. Surrounding this is a skirt of swept-back hot pink petals. It is compact crazy colourfulness.

WHAT TYPE? Anemone
HOW TALL? 90 cm (36 in.)
WHAT SPREAD? 40 cm (16 in.)
WHY GROW IT? Great for containers, perfect for small gardens, good garden variety

'Woodbridge'

This dahlia has won a Royal Horticultural Society Award of Garden Merit for its foliage, which is wonderfully divided, fern-like, and very rich green and glossy. The flowers are single and a simple lavender-pink, held on reddish stems high above the plant. Rather wonderful.

WHAT TYPE? Single
HOW TALL? 152 cm (60 in.)
WHAT SPREAD? 60 cm (24 in.)
WHY GROW IT? Great garden dahlia, stunning green foliage, perfect for pollinators

'Frigoulet'

Deep red and white in a bicoloured bloom could seem wrong on so many levels. Blood and bandages spring to mind. 'Frigoulet', however, is a rather marvellous small to medium flowered cactus. It can be a challenge to work such strong uncompromising colours into a planting plan—I admit that I don't even try. I grow it on its own in a large pot at the side of the house and thoroughly enjoy it.

WHAT TYPE? Cactus
HOW TALL? 152 cm (60 in.)
WHAT SPREAD? 60 cm (24 in.)
WHY GROW IT? Great garden dahlia, good dark green foliage, strong and striking flowers

'Akita'

This big lion's head of a dahlia has a flower form reminiscent of those huge chrysanthemums with layers and layers of incurved cupped petals. My grandmother used to love them. It's a blend of a range of colours from deepest reds and flame through to golden yellow and cream. Unlike other large flowered decoratives, the plant doesn't grow too tall, so it's well worth growing as a statement dahlia in a border display.

WHAT TYPE? Decorative chrysanthemum
HOW TALL? 100 cm (40 in.)
WHAT SPREAD? 60 cm (24 in.)
WHY GROW IT? Great garden dahlia, large and impressive blooms, bold colour blends

'Bee Happy'

An unusual colour combination of black foliage and purple-pink flowers. I haven't come across a collerette variety with such dark foliage before. I really like this one. I think it is rather special. The blooms are about 10 cm (4 in.) across, lilac-pink blending suddenly to cherry-burgundy-black near the centre, with a very small collar of deep pink petals just visible. It has great foliage and stems.

WHAT TYPE? Collerette
HOW TALL? 100 cm (40 in.)
WHAT SPREAD? 60 cm (24 in.)
WHY GROW IT? Great garden dahlia, perfect for pollinators, large and impressive blooms, dark black foliage

'Be A Sport'▲

This is a sport of 'Candy Cane'. It is variegated and has a splotch of white at the tips of the petals. It's quite a curious novelty dahlia.

WHAT TYPE? Decorative
HOW TALL? 90 cm (36 in.)
WHAT SPREAD? 60 cm (24 in.)
WHY GROW IT? Fun garden dahlia, talking point, curiously cute

'Fusion'▸

A fantastic upright decorative with the palest lilac-pink and white flowers that are set off brilliantly by the dark colour of the foliage. A very strong, compact, and floriferous variety. Perfect for containers and small gardens. Winner of a Royal Horticultural Society Award of Garden Merit.

WHAT TYPE? Decorative
HOW TALL? 80 cm (32 in.)
WHAT SPREAD? 60 cm (24 in.)
WHY GROW IT? Great garden dahlia, perfect for containers, great flower and foliage contrast

'Hot Cakes' ▼

To end with, an eccentric duo of anemone varieties. 'Hot Cakes' has outer burnt orange petals tipped with a soft orange. The pincushion centre is dark fiery red, making it incredibly striking on dark green foliage. It's floriferous, but dead-head to keep it blooming. 'Ryecroft Jim' ▶, the taller variety, is a hot cherry pink and clashing yolk yellow anemone explosion with glossy green foliage; it is winner of a Royal Horticultural Society Award of Garden Merit. Both are crazy colour combinations, but these dahlias are such fun to grow. The blooms transform from one day to the next as they mature. It's quite a floral metamorphosis. I'm getting more and more hooked, and at the moment it seems like there are lots of exciting new anemone varieties being introduced, particularly in the United States. I love them for all their queerness. These blooms will definitely stand out in your garden.

WHAT TYPE? Anemone
HOW TALL? 100–152 cm (40–60 in.)
WHAT SPREAD? 50–70 cm (20–28 in.)
WHY GROW THEM? Great garden dahlias, crazy colour combinations, fabulous and fun to grow

SEED MIXTURES

Dahlia seed mixtures come in all sorts of heights, flower forms, and foliage colours. My favourites are the dark-leaved types, such as 'Diablo' and 'Redskin'. Of all these varieties, however, 'Bishop's Children' remains my top pick. I've also become keen on a short collerette mix called 'Dandy' (sometimes sold as 'Yankee Doodle Dandy') and a very dwarf, small-flowered double dahlia mix with the simple and unsurprising name of 'Dwarf Double Mixed'. This last variety grows quickly and easily, and it makes perfect little dahlia plant packages to give as presents.

If you're on a tight budget, dahlias from seed are a great option. You don't need to limit yourself to the smaller, shorter plants—you can grow the bigger types of dahlia from seed too. Seed mixtures of 'Cactus Hybrids' (sometimes sold as 'Clangers Mix'), 'Giant Hybrids', 'Pompon Mixed', and 'Showpiece Mixed Hybrids', to name just a few, are easy to find and just as simple to grow as the more compact dwarf bedding types. You tend to get an extremely variable range of plants, but that's what makes it fun. I grew some 'Cactus Hybrids' seed that gave me plants varying from 90 cm (36 in.) to 180 cm (72 in.) tall. All sorts of colours, cactus-flower types, and foliage forms were represented. I'm sure none would have won any prizes at exhibition, but they were colourful, they flowered for months, they brought me total joy—and they cost just a few pence per plant to grow. Seed mixtures really are perfect to help spread the dahlia message to friends and family for next to nothing.

'Bishop's Children'

A fantastic dark-leaved mixture that can produce plants of quite different heights. It has a joyous colour range, and you're bound to find a favourite to save and propagate.

WHAT TYPE? Singles and semi-doubles
HOW TALL? 60–75 cm (24–30 in.)
WHAT COLOUR RANGE? Strong, fiery shades of red, orange, yellow, and pink
WHY GROW IT? Perfect for pollinators, good dark foliage, good border-sized plants

'Dandy' ▸

SYNONYM 'Yankee Doodle Dandy'

Bees and other pollinating insects adore this mixture of bright, bushy, dwarf collerettes with jolly colour combinations.

WHAT TYPE? Collerette
HOW TALL? 60 cm (24 in.)
WHAT COLOUR RANGE? Mainly deep and pale pink, red, orange, cream, and yellow
WHY GROW IT? Perfect for pollinators, great for containers

'Figaro' ◂

Strong bushy plants and good consistency of plant size. Breeders have made improvements to this mixture, so it is sometimes sold as 'Amore', 'Rigoletto', or 'Rigoletto Improved'. 'Figaro' can be the earliest and longest to flower from seed.

WHAT TYPE? Doubles and semi-doubles
HOW TALL? 30 cm (12 in.)
WHAT COLOUR RANGE? Full range, often available as mixed or single shades—orange, red, deep pink-violet, white, yellow
WHY GROW IT? Early bloomer, long blooming season

'Redskin'

'Redskin' is a good bet if you like dark-leaved dahlias. The foliage is not as dramatic as 'Bishop's Children' (more bronze than black), but the plants are more compact and consistent in terms of height.

WHAT TYPE? Doubles and semi-doubles
HOW TALL? 38 cm (15 in.)
WHAT COLOUR RANGE? Mainly red, orange, flame, yellow, and cream
WHY GROW IT? Good compact variety, perfect for containers

'Diablo'

A dwarf variety, with bright coloured double blooms. The foliage is more deep dark green than bronze to my eyes, but the richness of it sets off the flowers really well.

WHAT TYPE? Mainly doubles with some semi-doubles
HOW TALL? 30 cm (12 in.)
WHAT COLOUR RANGE? Range of red, orange, yellow and pink
WHY GROW IT? Bronze-green foliage, good compact variety

'Fireworks Mixed'

Few striped mixtures are offered, so this is an exciting development. Bright, jolly single blooms with splashes of contrasting colour look like dwarf dahlia-ripple ice-cream cones. Love it.

WHAT TYPE? Singles
HOW TALL? 40 cm (16 in.)
WHAT COLOUR RANGE? Striped or variegated blooms in shades of red, yellow, cherry pink, orange, magenta, and cream
WHY GROW IT? Striped flowers

'Dwarf Double Mixed'▸

'Dwarf Double Mixed' is a dainty miniature variety that grows well in small pots. The perky range of plants you get is very similar to another good dwarf seed mixture, 'Southbank Mixed' ▾.

WHAT TYPE? Doubles and semi-doubles
HOW TALL? 20–26 cm (8–10 in.)
WHAT COLOUR RANGE? Solid colours and blends of yellow, cream, pink, orange, red, and white
WHY GROW THEM? Perfect sized plants for a window box

GROWING AND PROPAGATING

Dahlia tubers come in all shapes and sizes. Some are similar to a clutch of new potatoes on a stick, while others are more cigar-like and spidery.

Dahlias are such easy plants to grow from seed, cuttings, or tubers, and you don't need to be an expert gardener to achieve an incredible display.

Getting to Know Tubers

Dahlia tubers are underground fleshy roots similar to bulbs. However, tubers are not as robust as the bulbs of tulips, daffodils, hyacinths, lilies, and other summer-flowering plants. Tubers can look quite octopus-like, and many growers refer to their individual parts as *chicken legs*. These "limbs" can break off quite easily, so always handle them carefully. Take extra special care with the crown, where the swollen, fleshy, underground parts meet the tuber's main stem or stems. To grow, dahlia tubers must have viable growing points, called *eyes*, at the crown.

Now that dahlias are becoming popular again, many garden centres and nurseries are offering fully grown flowering plants in the summer months. The advantage of shopping at this time is that you can see exactly what you're buying. However, you can pay double, triple, or even four times the cost of a tuber or rooted cutting purchased earlier in the year. If you are going to invest, look for strong, healthy, vibrant plants with lots of flower buds. Avoid any with mottled leaves, which could be a sign of a virus.

In terms of value for your money, tubers are great. If you are growing dahlias for the very first time, they will be a wonderful start to your adventures. But remember that dahlia tubers are not frost hardy. If you buy them in the winter or spring, you'll need a greenhouse or another warm, light, frost-free place in which to grow them. Before I invested in my lean-to greenhouse, I grew dahlias on a warm kitchen windowsill. You can plant them in the garden after the risk of frost has passed.

CHOOSING TUBERS

Be picky and examine tubers carefully. They should be dry, but also firm, fleshy, and almost potato-like. Look for little buds, also called *eyes*. The eyes are going to develop into shoots on the crown of the tuber at the base of the main stems; they are the stumpy bits to which all the parts are connected. At first, buds are very small and resemble the tiny eyes on a potato. They are not always easy to spot, although the tubers packed in individual clear plastic bags, which you can find at many garden centres, often have a few pinky white ones just starting to sprout.

Tubers come in all shapes and sizes. Some varieties just naturally make much bigger, fatter tubers, so don't be put off by the smaller ones. As long as they're not too dry and shrivelled, they should be fine. Avoid any that look completely desiccated, have broken up into lots of pieces, or are soft.

The region where the stem and tubers join is called the *crown*. This is where you can find the tiny eyes that give rise to shoots.

Bits of broken-off tuber are unlikely to grow into a plant unless they have some of the crown (stem base) attached with an eye on it. This may seem strange to anyone new to growing dahlias, as random bits of potato tubers will usually root and start a new plant. However, potatoes are *stem* tubers, so each potato is effectively a bit of swollen stem with potential growing points across its surface. Dahlias, however, are *root* tubers, so the bits of fat, fleshy tuber are just swollen bits of root, and without an area of stem where "eyes" or growing points originate, the fleshy root tuber simply cannot grow.

Tubers obtained from specialist growers and nurseries are best. They are the experts, and I've always been more than pleased with the tubers I've received from them. It's worth paying a little extra for the range, variety, and quality of tuber material. I also like to snap up bargain pre-packaged tubers at garden centres. Occasionally I've been very unlucky and a variety hasn't turned out to be the dahlia pictured on the label. This can be annoying, but it's the risk of buying any plant that's not in flower. When it comes to getting amazing value for your money, pre-packaged tubers are hard to beat. At heart, I love a good buy, so despite the odd unexpected variety popping up, I recommend them.

I wait until the first shoots break through the surface of the compost before I give potted tubers a thorough watering.

PLANTING TUBERS

If frosts have passed, you can plant dry tubers directly in the ground, but I prefer to start them in a pot, where they are protected from predators. If you do decide to plant them directly outside, note that the local slug and snail population can literally hear you placing tubers in the ground. By the time those first fresh dahlia shoots are sprouting, the slugs and snails from surrounding gardens have a common goal of homing in on your beloved plants and eating the entire lot. I am only slightly over-exaggerating. Never, ever plant dahlia tubers directly into the ground without implementing some sort of protection strategy against slugs and snails (see pages 210–212). Otherwise those first poor dahlia shoots are just sitting ducks.

Some dahlia growers advise soaking very dry tubers in water before planting. When it comes to moisture, I tread carefully and wait for shoots to appear before applying much water. At times I have gotten over-excited and lavished slightly too much water on a tuber of a brand-new variety I've finally managed to obtain. It then immediately sulked in its pot and rotted away in front of me. I now gently coax tubers into growth with warmth and lightly watered compost. Keep them moist for the first few weeks until growth is well under way.

It's important to label dahlias as you plant. This is easy to do: Simply push a small pencil-written label in close to the tuber. (I sometimes use larger labels hidden among the foliage for easy reference, but my dogs think pulling them out and chewing them is the most fun activity in the world.) When it's time to lift the tuber in late autumn, when it's all mud and sticks after cutting back your plants, you will have a record of which variety is which when you plant it again the following spring.

If you're potting tubers individually, don't over-pot them. Choose a container just a little bigger than the tuber when you're starting plants into growth, then plant out. You can grow your tubers in pretty much any free-draining, multi-purpose compost. Cover with moist compost, add a label, and—it bears repeating—wait for the first tiny shoots before watering thoroughly.

You now have a choice. You can just grow the plant and gaze in amazement at how many shoots it throws up and how rapidly they grow, or you can harvest a few cuttings to make new plants. If you want to grow the plant to a size that is ready for planting out, then after the shoots appear, pinch out the tips to encourage lots of branching.

Some specialist nurseries and collections sell rooted cuttings rather than tubers. Cutting material grows very vigorously, so I highly recommend it as a good way to start off a collection of plants. You can obtain quite a few varieties at once for little expense. Think carefully about the date you want cuttings delivered, as you'll need to unpack and pot them up immediately, then give them warmth and light on a sunny window or in a frost-free greenhouse. Once they've established, pinch them out to ensure good branching.

Caring for Young Plants

As soon as young plants and sprouting tubers are established and well rooted in their pots, it's best to grow them in quite cool temperatures. About 10° to 15°C (59°F) is adequate, and for the dwarf-bedding dahlias, even slightly cooler, well-ventilated conditions will result in sturdier plants. If temperatures get too high, the plants grow tall with soft, floppy foliage and lanky stems that struggle to support the flowers. Keeping the plants on the cool side, with good ventilation, encourages strong, stocky growth.

It's vitally important to wait until frosts have passed before planting outside, and ideally dahlias will benefit from hardening off before planting begins. This means acclimatizing the plants to outdoor conditions by cooling down temperatures for three to four weeks before planting time. If you can, keep plants in a well-ventilated cool greenhouse or in a cold frame. If you don't have either of these, putting plants on a tray and placing them outside (only on frost-free days) in the weeks before planting will help them to grow accustomed to the outside. Bring them back inside at night, when temperatures can dip drastically. If plants do get lightly frosted, quickly wash the frost off with water as soon as you can and you may save them.

Planting Out

Dahlias are thirsty, hungry plants that respond well to lots of watering and feeding. It's traditional to grow them in a separate border altogether, and many experts argue that dahlias need their own dedicated bed to achieve their best. I have a very small garden, and it's just not an option to give dahlias their own special place. They need to join the garden party and mingle. Dahlias are my favourite flowers, so I want them to entertain in my borders and in containers—pretty much everywhere the sun hits for a decent amount of time throughout the summer and autumn. Dahlias work for me in the same way spring bulbs do. Some come up in the same situation year in and year out, some I plant fresh every year, and some I use to create new and different container displays around doorways, sitting areas, and focal points in the garden.

Dahlias thrive in warm, open, sunny situations that don't dry out excessively during the hot summer months. They won't be happy in thin, poor soils, but they can also sulk when planted in heavy, cold, waterlogged conditions with little drainage. If you have concerns about your soil, incorporate lots of garden compost or well-rotted manure where you're going to place your plants, and add a little grit or sand to open up heavy soils. It's also well worth adding a light sprinkling of organic fertilizer, like pelleted chicken manure or bonemeal, at planting out time. But don't go wild with it, as too much nitrogen is not a good thing.

I plant dahlias a bit like roses—slightly deeper in the ground than the level they are in the pot. I also try to create a slight dip around the plant to retain moisture after watering in the warm summer months. If you're not sure how much space to give your plant, how big the hole should be, or how much garden compost to incorporate, my advice is simple: be generous. That said, half a small bucket of manure per plant is plenty. At planting out time I sprinkle half a handful of chicken manure pellets around each plant. This extra boost of nitrogen is just enough to fuel leafy growth for the first few weeks.

The roots of young plants should be well established in the pot and look healthy and eager to get growing. Unless plants are completely pot bound it's not necessary to tease the roots when planting.

I like to use rusty metal plant supports in the garden to provide a sturdy framework for my plants to grow up through.

Staking and Supporting

If you stake early, you will thank yourself in the long run. I advise staking when you plant. I'm not a fan of the traditional arrangement of three or four bamboo canes or dahlia stakes around each plant. It may be great for professional growers who need to carefully tie in lots of stems and keep a close eye on blooms, but if supports are going to be visible in the garden, they should add something to the overall display. Old, split bamboo canes can become perfect earwig hotels, so avoid these. Many growers now use solid green plastic canes, which last much longer. These are practical, but not that easy on the eye.

I prefer to see birch or hazel branches pushed into the soil all around the plant to provide a loose supporting structure. (You can also use this method with other tall herbaceous plants.) I like the look of rusted metal structures, and in recent years I have started investing in them. These are often sold as rose, delphinium, or peony supports, but they can work well with dahlias too. You can get a lifetime of use out of them, so they are quite affordable in the long term.

Tying up lots of plants across the spring and summer months isn't my idea of fun, and I struggle to find enough time to do it. Over the years I've refined my choice of varieties, and now I tend to grow those that need slightly less fuss and minimal support. My method is the lobster pot approach: put the structure or supports in place at planting, and let the plants grow up through them. I keep an eye out for vigorous shoots, and sometimes tie a few within the structure as the plants begin to put on growth. I can cope with a few floppy stems and plants growing into or among each other. It's a less formal, low-maintenance approach to staking for anyone who is short on time in the summer months.

The opposite approach is to support the plant in a way that completely hides the staking. I have seen this done brilliantly in borders in a number of gardens. Plants are grouped together, usually three around a central sturdy stake, and the main thick, central stems of each plant are tied to the stake with jute string. The surrounding side stems of the three plants hide the stake as they grow, and when the plants reach flowering height, they completely conceal their supports.

Dahlia 'Teesbrooke Redeye'

If you're going to grow dahlias exclusively in a bed or border, erecting a solid framework for the plants to grow up through can save a lot of time later in the year.

If you are going to grow all your dahlias in one big bed, such as for cutting purposes, I suggest erecting a framework above the plants that they can grow through. Ideally this will allow for adjustments as the plants grow taller. A simple grid made from stakes and wire mesh works well. The thin green plastic mesh usually sold by the metre at garden centres is also good, but it doesn't last as long. You can stretch the mesh between supports and add various tiers to give support at different heights.

Watering and Feeding

Dahlias are some of the thirstiest plants in the garden. If you don't already have water butts, also known as rainwater tanks, I strongly recommend installing them. You can't beat rainwater. It's aerated, it's at just the right temperature, and it's free. Dahlias can develop mildew in wet years, so it's always best to water plants at the base rather than overhead, although an occasional overhead foliar drench with an organic liquid feed will perk up lackluster foliage. I use a cup of my own comfrey tea (see page 216) mixed with organic seaweed feed in a 7.5-litre (2-gallon) can of rainwater. It has the extra benefit of very mild insecticidal and fungicidal properties.

It's a good idea to mulch around your dahlias, whether planted in the ground or in pots. These plants hate to dry out at the roots, so mulch will help prevent moisture from evaporating from the soil and will also suppress weeds. Well-rotted manure, leaf mould, or garden compost will also add humus to the soil. In pots, a thick layer of grit or gravel gives extra stability to container displays.

It's quite simple to feed dahlias. No matter how much you think you're giving them, your dahlias are probably pleading, *'Please, sir, I want some more'*. If you want lots of flowers from your plants, you have to give them lots of food—but it needs to be the right sort of food. I don't bother with much high-nitrogen fertilizer or feeds. There should be enough goodness in the soil to promote early green growth. (My own special brew of comfrey, nettle, and seaweed, mentioned above, is more a tonic to get the whole garden on track for summer.) If you are convinced that your soil is just not good enough or you haven't been able to improve it with compost or well-rotted manure, an all-purpose fertilizer applied in the first few weeks after planting out can help plants get established. I use a light sprinkling of organic chicken manure pellets to provide my young freshly planted dahlias with a hit of nitrogen for initial leafy growth. Remember that too much nitrogen can result in weak and floppy stems, small or no blooms, way too much leaf growth, and tubers that don't store well over the winter.

A simple garden arrangement featuring *Alchemilla mollis*, *Centranthus ruber*, ivy, fennel, and *Dahlia* 'Hamari Rose'.

Long, pointed buds will need dead-heading to encourage flowering to continue.

Dahlias need high-potash and high-phosphorous fertilizers. Most fertilizers have three numbers on the back of the package. These represent the ratio of nitrogen, phosphorous, and potassium, or N–P–K. You want a product where the last two numbers are as high as—or, ideally, higher than—the first, such as 5–10–10 or 10–20–20. Often these products are labelled as tomato or vegetable fertilizers, but some are specifically designed to encourage super duper flowering. General organic fertilizers can vary hugely in their N–P–K composition, but as a very rough guide, fish, blood, and bone is about 5–5–6, poultry manure is around 3–2–2, and horse manure is 1–0–1. I prefer organic liquid fertilizers.

Potassium and phosphorous break down quite slowly, so don't delay in using these fertilizers. You want the nutrients to be readily available during peak blooming. I start to use them about four weeks after planting and then regularly throughout the flowering season. A good drink with a can of diluted organic tomato feed once a week keeps them happy and flowering well into the autumn. No matter which fertilizers you decide to use, always follow the instructions and apply the amount stated on the packaging.

Encouraging Blooms

Professional dahlia growers and exhibitors go to great lengths to produce the very best dahlia blooms possible. They could write a whole book dedicated to the subjects of pinching out, disbudding, stopping, and removing side shoots. Removing these side buds and shoots concentrates the plant's efforts on producing a bigger and better bloom, so if that's your goal, go forth and disbud to your heart's content. For me, however, the adage "less is more" has always been something of an anathema. When it comes to my favourite flowers, more is clearly more. I admire perfection, but I just don't have time for it. So apart from nipping out the tips of my plants early in the season to encourage side branching, I don't bother removing side shoots or buds.

If you don't do any pinching out, it's not a complete disaster, but you will probably regret your decision later in the year. You may end up with lots of dahlia one-stemmed wonders; that is, plants that are flowering from a tall, central-dominating shoot. If you want to grow dahlias that produce lots of flowers for as long as possible, you'll probably get rather good at dead-heading. If you don't dead-head regularly, your plants will start to put all their efforts into producing seed and making tubers—essentially, getting ready to pack up early and have a snooze away from the rigors of blooming. However, if you remove spent blooms regularly and continue feeding with high-potash fertilizer, they'll keep going for months.

Use sharp florist scissors to dead-head. Look for blooms about to blow, as well pointy, squishy, beak-like buds. Be careful and observant. Don't cut off any of the tight round buds, as these haven't yet flowered. On a number of the compact shorter container varieties, just a few centimetres from the spent flower there may be a small leaf and another bud or two just waiting to develop. It's not always necessary to remove the main flower stem back to the base on these varieties. You can add all spent buds and blooms to the compost heap.

My advice is to not worry too much or get overly hung up on the non-hardy nature of dahlias. A slightly more relaxed approach frees you up to start being more creative with dahlias in different garden situations.

Overwintering Tubers

Dahlias are tender perennials, half-hardy at best, so in colder regions they cannot be left outdoors in winter. Generally, they are considered safe year-round in USDA zone 8 and above, with some tubers cold hardy to zone 7. Elsewhere, say, in zones 4 through 6, they can be and are grown, but they require protection in winter.

Because dahlias are not frost hardy, some gardeners have filed them away under "too much hard work." Lifting, cleaning off, prepping, and storing tubers can be too much of a chore for some. Hardiness, however, is really a sliding scale. It is defined as the ability to endure difficult conditions, and when talking about dahlias, we are specifically talking about very cold and very wet winter weather. Dahlia tubers have little innate ability to endure very long periods of cold, wet, frosty weather, but that can be helped—to an extent. If you live in a region or zone where your winters are not too severe, with only occasional hard frosts, there are things you can do to tip the scales of success in your favour. Plant your tubers quite deeply and on top of a layer of grit, and ideally in an area of your garden that is sunny, open, and in ground with good drainage. Apply a thick layer of mulch and maybe even some protection from an upturned plant pot at the soil surface to divert winter rain away from the tuber below the soil. You may find yourself amazed at how many of your dahlias make it through a cold winter left in the ground.

I use a generous layer of spent compost and sometimes a small sheet of black plastic just underneath the surface of the mulch. In very wet gardens with heavy soils, planting with plenty of grit and sand around the tubers and using grit or gravel as winter mulch can also produce excellent results. Winter wet is often the greater enemy than winter cold.

If you are going to lift plants, wait until frosts blacken the foliage in late autumn to allow maximum time to make tubers.

I must admit that, at the other end of the scale, I have had winters where I have gone to the trouble of lifting, cleaning, drying off, and storing tubers only to find that I've either dried them out too much or lost tubers to storage rot. To add insult to injury, in the spring I have then noticed that tubers I'd completely forgotten to lift have come into growth. There they are, stronger than ever, sending up copious green shoots and ready to give any plant in my borders a run for its money.

In cold, harsh, very wet winters, I've been unlucky and lost a lot of tubers. However, over the past 15 years this has happened only twice. I've learned to relax a little more and, apart from the varieties I absolutely can't live without or those that are too difficult or expensive to source, I cut back hard, mulch mulch mulch, and take my chances.

My advice is to not worry too much or get overly hung up on the non-hardy nature of dahlias. A slightly more relaxed approach frees you up to start being more creative with dahlias in different garden situations. New plants are relatively inexpensive and quick to grow and establish, so look at a rotten old tuber not as a loss, but as an opportunity to grow something new or re-invigorate your stock.

TO LIFT OR NOT TO LIFT

As summer sinks into autumn and the nights grow longer and colder, it's time to decide on a strategy for getting your dahlias through the winter. Don't do anything until the first hard frosts, which will blacken the foliage. Tuber formation often happens throughout late summer and well into autumn, right toward the end of the season. You want to make sure you've given your plants ample opportunity to make the biggest and best tubers they can. Now it is time to tidy the plants and cut back the stems to about 10 cm (4 in.) high. Next comes the rather critical decision of whether to lift your tubers.

If you live in an area that has very cold, wet winter weather and wet soils, or suffers from long hard frosts for days on end, you dahlia tubers will most likely freeze and die if you don't lift them. In places with warm, mild, dry winters and dry soils, with hardly any frost days, a layer of thick mulch will often be enough to see your tubers through safely (and if you mix in some organic slug

pellets with the mulch, even better). For those of us living in temperate climates somewhere between these two extremes, it may simply come down to considering how bad the forecast is for the coming winter—and how much time you have. If you have a lot of plants, it can be quite a task to lift all your tubers, clean and dry them off, dust with sulphur powder, pack them up, and find a cool, dark, frost-free location to store them.

Another factor to take into account is that not all dahlia varieties are abundant tuber makers. Some produce only very small, slender, cigar-like tubers, or tubers that look like a disappointing harvest of tiny new potatoes. These types are far more likely to dry out and shrivel up completely once lifted. If you decide to lift them, you need to keep them very slightly moist to stop desiccation. This means treading a fine line between not too wet and not too dry, and keeping them free of storage rots.

Some dahlia varieties have tubers that seem to be slightly more frost tolerant than others, so I'm afraid there's no hard-and-fast rule that fits all. You have to consider all the factors, then make your choice and take your chances. I make my dahlia decisions according to the following criteria:

1. I leave in the ground any dahlias I've grown from seed, varieties that I can obtain new plants of easily and cheaply, and those that are notoriously poor at making good-size tubers. I cut the stems down to ground level, and I use a generous amount of spent compost, with some organic slug pellets mixed in, as mulch. I apply the mulch to about 5 cm (2 in.) deep.
2. I bring into the greenhouse dahlia varieties I grow in pots and containers, and I lay the pots on their sides. I keep the plants frost free and allow them to dry out very gradually over the winter. In early spring I unearth the tubers, divide them, and re-plant in fresh compost.
3. I lift and store varieties that are very costly or difficult to replace.

LIFTING, PROTECTING, AND STORING TUBERS

The first step of lifting tubers is to cut back and clear away the blackened foliage, leaving just the main stems as a series of stumps about 10 cm (4 in.) high. Use a garden fork to gently ease and lift the soil around the perimeter of the plant. Don't shove your fork deep and hard into the soil. Be careful, and pretend you're lifting a crop of gourmet potatoes. Lift the tuber completely out of the ground, keeping it all in one piece if possible. Broken off bits of tuber won't grow without a piece of crown and a bud intact.

Next, tie a plastic label to the base of the chunkiest main stem. Do this as soon as you lift each individual variety. Don't wait until they're all out of the ground. At first, each tuber looks very distinctive and you'll convince yourself you will remember which one is which. You won't, and you'll probably end up cursing yourself in front of what looks like a lineup of muddy rejects from the local knobbly veg competition.

On sandy and loamy sites the soil will often fall away easily from around a tuber, but on clay soils you will need a brush to loosen and remove much of it. Hold a tuber firmly by the main stems and be careful not to damage the crown area while loosening the soil or carrying the clump. A tuber with a cracked or broken crown will generally not grow, so be extra careful with this top part.

Tubers grown in quite heavy clay soils will often hold together well when lifted out of the ground.

It is not necessary to clean off every bit of soil with a hose before drying the tubers. I remove any big clods of soil and give the tubers a general brushing off. Afterwards, ideally leave them upside down for two or three days on the staging in the greenhouse, or anywhere dry and frost free. Residual moisture in the hollow main stems will slowly drain out. You can help this process by using a knife or screwdriver to pierce a hole through the hollow stems. Once the tubers have been dried off, it should be easier to brush away the rest of the soil or compost. Before putting them to bed, check over the tubers. Use sharp florist scissors to cut off any damaged or soft bits that are diseased or rotting. At this stage you can trim back the main stems to about 5 cm (2 in.)

Next, dust all the tubers with green or yellow sulphur powder. This will help prevent storage rots and fungal infections. Then place each tuber on some newspaper or brown packaging paper; cover with wood shavings, wood chips, or compost; and scrunch and wrap the paper around the tuber. Put the dahlia packages in an old cardboard box. Don't pack them too tightly, however. Think of them as mini hibernating mammals that still need a little room to breathe.

If you're going to store your dahlias in a location that is slightly warmer and airier than a garage, outbuilding, or loft, your tubers could dry out too much if you follow the

After a thorough dusting with sulphur powder, I use wood shavings to cover tubers and then wrap brown paper around the tuber.

method above. Instead, pack your tubers in a box and cover them with moist compost or coarse sand to save them from desiccation.

I place some of my tubers in a cold closet under the stairs, and some in the loft. There's no special heating in either location, but both are adjacent to a warm, centrally heated house. The conditions are cold, dry, and dark, but frost-free. These are the essential requirements for the tubers. Too warm and your tubers may try to sprout back into growth, or they may shrivel up completely. Too damp and fungal rots can have a field day. Tubers can dry out too much over the winter, but I find this is rarely an issue if they are lifted as late as possible in autumn, partially dried off, and kept cool enough. I have tried packing tubers in moist compost, but I lost quite a few to storage rot. Wood shavings and paper work better for me. You may need to experiment to discover the best method for you.

Ideally, check the tubers once a month for any signs of rot. I usually forget until the worst of the winter months are over. Most years the majority of the tubers come through just fine.

POT TUBERS

If digging up and storing dahlia tubers each year feels too much like hard work, or if you simply don't have the time, there is another way to overwinter your favourite plants. This method is also good for varieties that are late to mature or shy in terms of tuber production.

During late spring or early summer, take cuttings from your dahlias. Plant them into 12.5 cm (5 in.) pots, give them high-potash fertilizer, and water as usual. Pinch out all the flower buds. All the nutrients that are normally used to produce fabulous flowers need to be forcefully re-directed into making big, healthy tubers. Confined to their pots and

Secrets of the Professionals: Perfecting the Art of Winter Storage

PROFESSIONAL DAHLIA GROWERS and breeders have gone to great lengths to discover the very best ways to store tubers over the winter period. Many thoroughly clean their tubers with water, completely removing all the soil. However, others prefer to keep their tubers as dry as possible throughout the process, and they use compressed air to carefully clear away all the compost. Some experts report that cleaning with compressed air instead of water significantly increases the success rate of storing tubers over the winter, with losses down to less than 1 percent.

Tuber cuttings

Either way, cleaned tubers are often dusted with sulphur or sprayed with a liquid fungicide and covered with coarse horticultural sand, wood chips, or wood shavings, then stored in the dark in cardboard or wooden crates at a constant cool temperature of about 6° to 7°C (42–45°F).

Some dahlia enthusiasts have gone even further and experimented with wrapping sections of very clean tubers in tight plastic wrap. This extreme but highly effective method does not use any wood shavings, newspaper, compost, or any storage material. The amount of room needed to store tubers is drastically reduced, and there is no need to check the tubers over the winter. However, the method is quite involved, and careful preparation is crucial. You must first thoroughly wash the tubers, then carefully divide them into sections. Each "limb" of tuber must have a section of the crown and at least one "eye." You must also use a fungicidal dip or drench to reduce the numbers of fungal spores present on the tubers. (Some experts use a dilute bleach liquid dip of one teaspoon of bleach per 4.5 litres [1 gallon] of water.) The tuber sections must be dry before you begin wrapping. All this careful preparation is vital for minimizing any rotting during storage.

Organic growers can dust the sections with sulphur by applying a very thin coating over the whole surface of the tuber. Gently shake the tuber sections individually in a plastic bag containing one tablespoon of sulphur powder to 20 tablespoons of vermiculite, perlite, or horticultural sand.

After the tubers have been divided, washed, labelled, and treated with a fungicide, dry them gently overnight at room temperature. Wrap the tubers the following day. Don't allow them to dry out too much. Wrap the tuber sections separately. They will look like individually wrapped cigars. Don't forget to label. You can then group them together in bundles using a further layer of plastic wrap or masking tape. Put them into cardboard boxes and store at around 7°C (45°F).

prevented from flowering, the poor dahlias can't do anything but produce tubers. This is particularly good for those varieties that are far too busy flowering in your borders to make time for tuber production. This way, they have no choice.

You can then easily overwinter these tubers snug inside their pots in a frost-free location like on the staging under the bench in a cold greenhouse. You can bring them into growth the following spring, and take more cuttings and produce more plants.

REVIVING TUBERS

When spring arrives, it is time to retrieve your tubers and start them into growth. Sadly, it's also the time when fungal spores suddenly become active. However, if any tubers are causing you concern, you can spray or drench them with an organic fungicidal solution. There are many organic recipes that work well and use the anti-fungal properties of garlic, lemons, cider vinegar, seaweed feed, baking soda, and more. I have used the following recipe with success: Into a 4.5-litre (1-gallon) watering can, add 4 tablespoons apple cider vinegar, 1 tablespoon vegetable oil, 1 tablespoon molasses, and ½ tablespoon baking soda. Fill with water, mix, and use as a one-time drench or spray.

Dealing with Pests, Diseases, and Disorders

Like many other garden plants, dahlias can be prone to pests, diseases, and disorders. Many will pose the same threat at the same time each year. If you know when problems are likely to be most troublesome, you can act quickly, catch them early, and overcome them relatively easily.

Dahlias suffer from slugs and snails, aphids (particularly blackfly and greenfly), caterpillars, and earwigs. Powdery mildew and fungal infections can be bad in very wet growing seasons, and viruses can be problematic on some plants. If you lift and keep tubers over the winter, storage rot can cause problems if tubers are unhealthy, are not dried off properly, or are not stored in cool, dry conditions.

Poor flowering can be caused by a number of things, such as overfeeding with nitrogen-rich fertilizer, or not feeding enough with high-potassium and high-phosphorous feeds. Too little sun, or keeping plants too dry at the roots, can also be detrimental to flower production. I am always looking for good homemade organic solutions, and more and more amateur dahlia lovers seem to be treading this path. However, if I have an extremely bad infestation I may resort to a specific one-time spot treatment with a chemical solution, but only when all organic options have failed.

SLUGS AND SNAILS

In a wet year you may have to battle slugs and snails. They love to hide in thick ivy, under old wooden planks, down the side of railway sleepers, under plant pots, and in the small spaces between plastic pots, trays, and modules. Young dahlia shoots and leaves are top on their list of gourmet treats, and some will munch flowers too. After a rain shower or

The telltale sign that slugs or snails have been at work is a trail of slimy residue across shoot tips and young leaves.

on a damp, humid night, they are particularly active. Never plant dahlias without a good dose of organic slug and snail pellets or a deterrent barrier—preferably both. There are lots of good organic pellets available. Some are made from sheep wool, while others contain ferric phosphate. Using beer traps to provide a slug-attracting watering-hole diversion is also a good tactic, as is a thick layer of broken eggshells or a dry, dusty mulch. (Note that dust mulches are less effective during a wet, rainy spring.) Caffeine is also effective at deterring slugs, so save old coffee grounds and spread them around your plants. Copper gives them a nasty shock, so copper tape is good for plants in containers. Or, if you're feeling flush, try a mulch of copper pennies.

My tactic is to place citrus peels around the garden in very early spring weeks before planting out time. The peels will attract lots of slugs and snails, in particular those tiny ones that hide in the soil. In the morning you will find them congregated underneath your fruit rinds, and you can dispose of the lot. Do this repeatedly and you will slowly reduce the population in your garden before it's time to plant out. If you use a combination of the citrus skin method, a barrier, and some organic pellets, you should win the fight. For those on a bit of a save-the-dahlia mission, head into the garden on a damp, drizzly evening with a flashlight and a small bucket. You'll catch them on any young emerging shoots.

Ants farm blackfly and other types of aphids on dahlias. They herd the aphids to the fresh young tips, flower buds, and young leaves of plants, where the aphids produce the sweetest honeydew—the sticky, sweet substance the ants are after. They can quickly transfer aphids to all of your plants, so it's important to act fast when you spot them.

APHIDS AND ANTS

All forms of aphids are bad news, but greenfly and blackfly can be a serious problem. They appear on young tasty growth, around flower buds, on shoot tips, and under leaves. If you're really unlucky, a small army of ants is farming them from one plant to another. (This is often the case with heavy infestations of blackfly.) Tackle the problem the moment you see it. In just a few days a plant can go from having a sprinkling to being totally plastered on every bud and growing point. Aphids are sapsuckers and can quickly spread viruses and distort growth.

I try to encourage a healthy population of ladybirds, as their larvae do a good job of feasting on aphids. But if you're suddenly under attack, use a hose to wash off any aphids before they reach epidemic levels. Organic insecticidal sprays can be effective, especially if you use them to spray plants in early spring. Young dahlia foliage is quite tender, so test your spray on a few leaves first. There are organic sprays available made from a huge range of naturally occurring oils or compounds that are toxic to aphids, including garlic, tomato leaves, chilli peppers, neem oil, and citrus oil. However, some can also harm the beneficial insects you want to encourage, so use a targeted approach. Spray as soon as you see your first aphid.

Ants feed on the sticky honeydew that aphids produce, so they farm and defend this precious resource. Tackle the ants first by mixing 2 heaped teaspoons of boric acid powder with 10 teaspoons sugar or honey and 2 cups of boiling hot water. Let it cool for an hour, and then spritz the solution at various places along the ant run. Remove any dahlia foliage that is near to or touching the ground, and spray the solution around the base of the main stems. The sweetness attracts the ants to the solution, and they spread it and feed it to others throughout the colony. The boric acid poisons their stomachs and affects their metabolism. Keep using the solution for a couple of weeks, even as the number of ants decreases. At first you may see an increase in activity, but this will drastically decline as the poison takes effect.

Boric acid may sound scary, but it's far more toxic to insects than mammals. (For humans, it's only slightly more toxic than table salt.) Achieving the right mix of boric acid is important. Too much will kill the ants before they reach the colony, but too little will not be effective. As with all pest and disease-control substances, exercise caution when using and always keep it away from children and pets, ideally in a tightly sealed, clearly labelled container.

If you have earwigs, during the day you'll usually see chewed petals—and occasionally the pincers of one as it scuttles away.

Once the ants are gone, remove the blackfly infestation by cleaning the affected parts of your plants with a dilute solution of organic insecticidal soap.

CATERPILLARS

All sorts of moth and butterfly caterpillars munch on dahlias. Many are active at night, and they can be tricky to spot. It's often best to wait until the sun goes down and use a torch to hunt for them, then collect, remove, and re-home. I pick them off, pop them into a container with a lid and a few leaves to munch on, and take them to the park on my morning dog walk, where I usually release them onto some nettles.

EARWIGS

Earwigs move in during blooming season. They chew holes in young foliage, petals, and flower buds, and they also put many people off growing dahlias at all. The sight of them wriggling out of petals and scuttling across the tablecloth is just too much. The forceps-like pincers at the base of their abdomens is frightening to behold, but they are pretty harmless to humans. Earwigs are essentially nocturnal scavengers, and during the day, like slugs and snails, they love to hide in moist, dark, snugly fitting places—particularly the tubular florets of dahlia blooms. Allegedly earwigs eat aphids and other garden pests, but I'm convinced they do so only after they've made a real mess of my favourite blooms.

Over the years I have used various traditional organic methods for dealing with earwigs, and I've been disappointed with the results. I have tried using traps of cut lengths of hose, rolled-up newspaper, and upturned plant pots stuffed with hay on top of canes. I have successfully caught many earwigs, but once I emptied the traps the lightning-quick pests were able to escape. I was beginning to think that controlling them organically was just not possible, but I may have solved the problem. I use two different traps that employ a sweet bait laced with boric acid powder. Both traps are similar to those designed to control ants.

For the first trap, paint the inside of a small clay pot with thick, slightly warmed molasses syrup. Sprinkle boric acid around the inside of the pot until the molasses is completely covered by a thin layer of the powder. Stuff the pot with shredded newspaper, hay, or straw. Place the upturned pot onto a cane next to a group of dahlia blooms. Earwigs should be lured inside by the molasses and moist environment, and they will become coated in boric acid as they tuck into a sticky treat. Empty the traps daily, ideally over a bucket of water so the earwigs drop into it and can't get away. Any earwigs that you don't get, or that somehow escape, will hopefully spread the boric acid–laced molasses to the rest of their brood.

The second type of trap is very similar. Mix 3 tablespoons of boric acid powder with 3 tablespoons of molasses and just a teaspoon or two of boiling hot water to help dissolve and mix the powder and molasses together and form a thick paste. Pour or paste the mixture into an empty tuna can or yogurt container until you have coated the inside with a thin layer. Fill with shredded paper, hay, or straw. Close the lid over the tin or container to keep the rain out, but leave a gap to allow the earwigs in. Glue to the top of a cane stopper and place near groups of dahlia blooms on the top of a cane or plant support. Keep these traps in place for a month or two.

Brown-headed vine weevil larvae look particularly gruesome and feed on the fine roots of many different plants. They like the free-draining conditions in containers, and they are often brought into the garden on the roots of container grown plants.

VINE WEEVILS

Adult vine weevils have a broad palate, and they will devour a variety of flowers in the garden. On my evening hunts for earwigs I often find vine weevils feeding on dahlia petals. I've also encountered the grubs when unearthing container-grown dahlias in early spring in my greenhouse. Vine weevils seem to be particularly troublesome if you grow a lot of plants in containers, as I do. However there is a good, if slightly costly, way to control them organically. In late spring and in the summer and early autumn I water my containers with clean water and nematodes, which are live microscopic worms. (You can order nematodes online.) Your soil must be above 5°C (41°F) and moist for nematodes to be able to move around, and you cannot let your containers dry out. The nematodes will kill vine weevil larvae within two to three weeks, so if you think you have a problem, start using this control as soon as soil temperatures warm up in mid-spring. Don't use a watering can with a fine rose, as the worms could get lodged in it and never reach the soil. It's more effective to water gently, but close to soil level, without any rose at all.

SPIDER MITES

In hot and dry conditions dahlias can suffer extensively from spider mites, which spin fine little webs across the underside of leaves, turning them yellow and brown in patches. If you get an outbreak, remove these infected lower leaves right away. The mite population can move quickly from leaf to leaf and from plant to plant.

Fine webs, tiny red brown mites, and yellow mottling are unmistakable signs of a spider mite infestation.

Powdery mildew often affects the older and lower leaves first. Always remove those worst affected and spray the whole plant with a dilute milk spray. Young growth will often overcome and grow through it. Don't put infected leaves on the compost heap.

My dahlias rarely suffer from this particular pest. I regularly water their foliage with a large can of rainwater containing three large cups of homemade comfrey tea. This acts as a great foliar feed and also wets and washes the foliage, and also repels all sorts of insects that love dry conditions. Comfrey can access nutrients deep in the soil using its extensive root system, so the plant's leaves and stems are naturally very rich in nitrogen, potassium, and phosphorous. These elements are the basis of most fertilizers and are essential for healthy plant development.

Ideally you want to grow *Symphytum ×uplandicum* 'Bocking 14', a type of Russian comfrey. This is a sterile variety, so it won't seed around your garden like wild comfrey. It's a valuable plant in the garden, and so easy to make into a liquid feed. Simply chop up the leaves and stems and cover with water inside a bucket with a close-fitting lid. (A bucket designed for holding used diapers is perfect.) Wait a few weeks, and be warned: it smells evil. After the tea has matured, you can make a fertilizer as good as many of the commercial brands. The homemade version is a free source of nutrients for your dahlias, and it also wards off spider mites and other aphids. Bristly comfrey leaves can irritate the skin, so wear gloves when cutting or handling the plant.

POWDERY MILDEW AND FUNGAL INFECTIONS

Powdery mildew is a blanket term for a number of species of fungi that infect all sorts of garden plants. As its name suggests, this is a grey-white, talcum powder–like fungus that often covers the lower leaves and stems of dahlias. The moist days and cool nights of late summer create an ideal climate for spore growth and dispersal, and powdery mildew can become quite unsightly and spread very quickly.

The key to prevention is growing plants in locations with good air circulation. Don't plant too densely and grow plants in full sun, as direct sunlight inhibits spore germination. Keep plants healthy and feed them well with organic tomato fertilizer or dilute comfrey tea. Always pick off the most badly affected plant parts, usually the oldest and lowest leaves, and put them straight into a rubbish bag, not on the compost heap.

In really bad years you can keep powdery mildew at bay by spraying with cow's milk. Mix 3 parts milk with 7 parts water, and use a spray bottle to drench both sides of the stems and foliage. Ideally, spray in late afternoon on a sunny day. Repeat every seven to 10 days until you have the mildew under control. Proteins in the milk interact with sunlight to create a brief fungicidal effect, as the sun breaks down the mildew spores and burns them off. Powdery mildew can often start to appear on dahlias in mid- to late summer, earlier in very wet years. Milk sprays work best when used preventively, before mildew can gain a strong foothold, so start before there are any signs of infection. And use low-fat milk—whole milk can result in stinky foliage! Commercial organic sprays containing sulphur or potassium bicarbonate also work well.

Virus symptoms can be quite subtle and hard to spot, but yellowing around the veins and in the middle of the leaf are classic signs that a plant has been infected.

VIRUSES

Several viruses can affect dahlias, and you should watch for a few obvious symptoms. If a plant's leaves look sickly and you can see yellowing along the veins or in the centre of the leaves, the plant likely has a mosaic virus. If the growth of a plant seems heavily stunted, or if the foliage is limp and has variegated markings and it seems to be permanently wilting, some sort of virus is at play.

Pull up and burn immediately any plants showing any signs of virus. Do not put them on the compost heap or you risk spreading the virus to other plants. If you can, thoroughly clean pots and the area where the virus-infected plant was growing.

CROWN OR LEAFY GALLS

I've only ever had crown or leafy gall on a dahlia plant a couple of times. It is bizarre to behold. At the base of the main stem, where it meets the tuber, a profusion of mini wart-like nodules or shoots appear. This is usually caused by bacteria entering a cut or damaged area on the tuber, which then grows and looks like an enlarged tumor. The cells at the base of the stem are triggered to multiply very quickly, resulting in an explosion of deformed and distorted tiny growths known as galls.

Dahlias for Beginners

'Baby Red'
'Bambino'
'Bishop of Llandaff'
'Classic Rosamunde'
'E Z Duzzit'
'Giggles'
'Happy Single Flame'
'Karma Fuchsiana'
'Lucky Ducky'
'Moonfire'
'Ryecroft Marge'
'Waltzing Mathilda'

Large-Flowered Dahlias

'Akita'
'Amber Banker'
'American Beauty'
'Bee Happy'
'Blue Bayou'
'Boogie Nites'
'Gitts Crazy'
'Happy Halloween'
'Jeanne D'Arc'
'Ripples'
'Sterling Silver'
'Thomas A. Edison'

Crown or leafy gall sometimes looks like an over-exuberant mass of tiny, healthy, leafy shoots at the crown of the tuber, hence the two names. Just like viral-stricken plants, those with crown or leafy gall have to go, as the bacteria can spread quickly to other plants. If the plant is growing in a pot, throw away the compost too, as it could be rife with bacteria, and wash the pot thoroughly in hot, soapy water.

This is the most extreme case of ring fasciation, or hen and chicks, I have ever encountered. Completely bizarre.

MUTATIONS AND FASCIATION

From time to time dahlias do the most unusual things. Every year I have at least one plant that throws up some bizarre growths: Medusa-like flower buds; thick, flattened, and fused stems; elongated or misshapen inflorescences; co-joined blooms; and varieties that change colour from the year before or send out strong shoots that bloom a slightly different shade. Sometimes it's hard to pinpoint the exact cause of these symptoms, but a number of factors can play a role.

The most common cause of bizarre growth is often a phenomenon referred to as *fasciation*, defined as a malformation of plant stems commonly manifested as enlargement and flattening as if several stems were fused together. Fasciation can be caused by random genetic mutations; viral infections; damage to the plant or tuber from frost, high temperatures, or chemicals; or even physical harm from insects or animals right at the growing tip. Often a bacterial infection from *Rhodococcus fascians* will also cause some of these symptoms. Abnormal activity right at the growing tip of the plant can produce fasciated flat stems or growths. Often an abnormal number of flowers are also produced on affected stems. However, completely normal branches or growth may then subsequently arise from these fasciated parts. *Ring fasciation* is where the central bud or flowerhead on a stem is surrounded by a ring of buds. Sometimes this is known as *hen and chicks*. Fasciation in dahlias is highly unpredictable but is often limited to a single stem. It won't necessarily occur the following year.

Small-Flowered Dahlias

'Bishop of Auckland'
'Bonne Espérance'
'Ginger Snap'
'Hootenanny'
'La Recoleta'
'Lauren Michele'
'Mexican Black'
'Nippon'
'Rock Star'
'Scura'
'Sweetheart'
'Tiny Treasure'

Award-Winning Dahlias

'Ann Breckenfelder'
'Bishop of Llandaff'
'David Howard'
'Dovegrove'
'Fascination'
'Hillcrest Royal'
'Magenta Star'
'Marie Schnugg'
'Moonfire'
'Omo'
'Twyning's After Eight'

The bizarre, alien-like growth of crown gall.

Colour changes—or, more correctly, colour mutations—are also quite common in dahlias. Some sort of damage to a dahlia's genetic code, usually in the cells right at the growing points, causes this to occur. Often there's a loss of part of the genetic code on a chromosome that causes a loss in a particular characteristic linked to colour.

Biologically active chemicals such as hormones and enzymes can cause this damage, as can toxic chemicals in the air or water. Background radiation, cosmic rays, x-rays, and UV light may also trigger mutations, but they can also happen completely naturally during a process called *crossover*, when cells divide and grow and the numerous chromosomes detach and then reform. The genes can become slightly mixed up or scrambled, and effectively the end part of one chromosome may be exchanged and then reattached to a different corresponding chromosome. The instructions to make the numerous proteins, sugars, and enzymes that are required to create the original colour of the dahlia are lost, which results in a change in the colour, hue, or saturation. The original colour may even be lost completely and a different underlying colour might be revealed. The end result of severe loss or change to the genetic code is usually white. Some dahlia varieties are more genetically delicate than others, and thus mutate or send out sports more often.

Propagating

Dahlias can be propagated from tubers, cuttings, and seeds. The first two methods produce a plant that is identical to the parent plant. Propagation by seed will yield plants that vary from the parent in colour, form, or other characteristics, but the possibility of discovering a new variety makes this option very attractive to many gardeners.

DIVIDING TUBERS

There are many different ways to divide tubers. You will get a more successful outcome if you divide the tuber just before starting it into growth, when you can clearly see the eyes on the crown, or as the new shoots are sprouting. Start at the crown, at the base of the main stem, and ensure each portion has a piece of crown with at least one or more eyes or shoots on it, as well as a leg (section of tuber) attached. Pot up each bit of tuber into a separate container with its section of stem and shoot intact. If kept warm and moist, each tuber cutting will soon establish roots. Don't over-water them. Grow the plants on and pinch out shoots to get a bushy branching habit.

Cock-A-Doodle Crazy Blooms—Colour Breaking in Dahlias

COLOUR BREAKING OCCURS when some petals within a dahlia flower are one hue and others are another, or when individual petals have flecks, splashes, and splotches. Given all the complex genetics and environmental factors that can trigger mutations in dahlias, it's no wonder this phenomenon occurs so readily.

As in many flowers, in dahlias genes play a vital part in the control and development of flower colour. A flower initially develops from a very small number of cells. During the development of the early blooms, some genes are turned on in parts of the flower bud, while in other parts they are switched off. When a gene is turned on can determine how much of the bloom acquires colour. Short periods of on-and-off gene activity can create streaks, splashes, splotches, or small areas of contrasting colour within a bloom. UV light and background radiation are also thought to influence this, and they can be integral in causing mutations to occur.

Dahlia 'Tamburo' was a solid deep red colour in its previous flowering season. After a harsh winter and a cold spring with late frost, it survived, but its blooms are now variegated deep red and white. It's likely that some sort of mutation occurred, but it's hard to determine the cause. These pure white patches could indicate a severe loss to its genetic colour code.

TAKING CUTTINGS

Tubers will start pushing up lots of shoots in just a couple of weeks if given plenty of warmth and light; around 20°C (68°F) will kick-start them into action. It's almost wasteful not to take cuttings from a healthy tuber. Young plants developed from rooted cuttings grow stronger and faster, and most decent-size tubers produce at least five shoots. That's lots of free plants for the taking. In general, plants grown from cuttings will start to flower slightly later, but they will last long into autumn.

Taking a few cuttings won't harm a healthy mother plant. However, if a tuber is very small or has very few eyes on its crown, or if you have gone to great lengths to obtain a chicken leg or tuber cutting, be careful not to exhaust it. Instead pot up, grow on, plant out, and feed and water well in the first season to build the plant up to make a robust tuber. The following year, you can increase stocks and go cutting crazy.

When shoots are about 5 to 8 cm (2–3 in.) long, they're the perfect size for cutting material. Fill large modules or small 8 cm (3-in.) pots with a good, open, free-draining compost. If compost seems too dense, mix in a little horticultural sand, fine grit, perlite, or vermiculite. Use a clean, sharp knife to cut the shoots carefully just above where they join the crown.

Trim the stem of the cutting to just below the first leaf joint under the lowest pair of leaves. Remove these lower leaves, and leave the rest of the cutting as it is. This area directly underneath a leaf node will callus over quickly and make roots. I dip the base of my cuttings in an organic rooting powder, then dib a hole with a pencil, place the cutting into the compost, and gently firm around the cutting. Sometimes I use one small plastic pot per cutting, and other times I place cuttings around the edge of a slightly bigger 18 cm (7 in.) terra-cotta pot, especially if I'm taking a number of the same variety.

Cuttings around the edge of a clay pot seem to root even more quickly, although most

Apart from a row of black-and-white *Dahlia* 'Twyning's After Eight', the rest of the dahlias in this mini trial display have been grown from seed. It took just three months for them to become mature flowering plants.

Viruses and the Importance of a Clean Knife

IT'S SO EASY to accidentally infect dahlia cuttings and other plants. A plant may not immediately exhibit signs of virus, particularly early in the year when you're busy taking lots of cuttings from sprouting tubers, so it's essential to clean your knife between every single cut. This might sound tedious, but it's easy. Simply keep a jar filled with hot water and a generous squirt of household bleach to one side. After each cut dip your cutting knife into the jar, then use a clean towel, with a few spots of bleach on it, to wipe. Before you know it, this action will become automatic.

I have to confess I didn't always do this in the first few years of growing dahlias. Sadly, I learned the hard way and spread dahlia mosaic virus to a number of plants and young cuttings, all of which had to be destroyed. If you don't like using bleach, vinegar or concentrated lemon juice are good organic alternatives.

You can accidentally transmit a virus from plant to plant when cutting flowers from plants. Make sure scissors are always clean and sharp. Maybe I'm over-cautious, but I keep a cloth in my pocket that has just a few drops of concentrated bleach on it. I use this to wipe my blades before cutting flowers from a different plant.

dahlia cuttings are so easy and keen to grow that any sort of container will be fine. I place my cuttings in a clear plastic bag and leave them in the greenhouse, but you could place them in a propagator or any warm light place. Keep them out of direct sunlight at first, though.

If I'm a little late making cuttings, and the material is slightly longer and leafier than I'd like, I take out the tip of the cutting and trim off a few of the leaflets. The cutting should be less water-stressed, as it has fewer leaflets to support. Once the cutting has made roots, the side shoots start to grow and the result is a stocky branched plant.

Cuttings should establish nicely in just a few weeks. If you can see white roots at the bottom of the pot, pot up your cuttings into a bigger container and, if you haven't already, carefully pinch out the main growing tip to encourage side shoots and a bushy habit. Don't delay, or you will end up with a very tall, lanky plant that will never make a great shape. Be cruel to be kind. Early pinching out results in much better, stockier, well-branched dahlias.

SOWING SEED

Growing plants from seed couldn't be easier. When I first had a go, I couldn't believe that such a substantial plant like a dahlia could grow from a tiny seed to an adult flowering plant in just one growing season. So when I produced around 50 'Bishop's Children' dark-leaved dahlias in my first attempt at growing from seed, I was quite amazed.

You can grow a great range of dahlias from seed, but this method is most popular with the dwarf-bedding type dahlias. In some ways, this dahlia is the shorter, even more floriferous cousin of the larger-named varieties. Parks departments often grow them in large quantities to fill flowerbeds with colour all summer long. They make great garden plants, as they are perfect for all kinds of containers and window boxes, and even for planting in vertical wall displays. For the home gardener they are an excellent type of dahlia with which to play. Dahlia seed is inexpensive and widely available, and as the flower's renaissance and re-discovery grows stronger, an ever-increasing variety of types is available.

Most dahlia seed varieties are mixtures. You will often get some slight variations in the form and colour of the flowers and foliage, as well as their overall size and habit

Creating Hybrids

DAHLIAS ARE ONE of the most capricious flowers in the garden. Their major overriding genetic disposition is mutable, changeable, unstable, or, as I like to call it, "floristically erratic." Even populations of species dahlias are naturally quite promiscuous and can be variable, so in some ways the incredible range of dahlia varieties we have today was almost inevitable. These inherently unstable characteristics make hybridizing dahlia varieties (essentially crossing one cultivar with another to breed new types) rather easy. It's also very quick, as in just one year you can cross two different flowers, collect and sow seed, and then grow the plants from seedlings to flowering adults. Most new dahlia varieties have been raised from seed at some stage following crossing, and there's absolutely no reason why you can't have a go at breeding and designing your own perfect plant. There are two very different approaches to this undertaking, and I rather like both.

You can sit back, put your feet up, and leave it to the bees and butterflies. Just remember, at the end of the season, to collect some nice big seed heads from a few of your favourite plants. Let the seed heads dry, then pull them apart and remove the seed. Sow it the following spring. You'll get a slightly different range of dahlias, I can assure you—different colours, different heights, different flower forms. They'll be pleasant enough plants, and considering the general lack of parental effort invested and the fact that they've cost you next to nothing, what's not to love?

Many top breeders and growers use a more targeted approach involving selected seed and pollen parents. This method just needs a bit more thought and input, but the potential to produce your dream dahlia becomes much more of a possibility.

Start with a clear mental picture of your ideal dahlia. It's time to refine your favourite qualities of the flower, and decide on the form, colour, size, and habit of the dahlia you like best and want to produce. Focus in on just one or two particular characteristics that you'd really love to come together in your dream dahlia, such as very dark foliage, deep claret petal colour, miniature anemone flower form, or tall, straight, and sturdy flower stems. Remembering your key characteristics or objectives is very useful when you are faced with lots of very pretty young dahlia seedlings that are flowering for the first time. You'll need to discard quite a number of them, so unless you have endless time and an enormous garden for growing all of them, stay true to your aim. Save only those that really show potential and the characteristics and qualities on which you've decided.

So which to choose as Dahlia Mum and Dahlia Dad (or, if you prefer, seed parent and pollen bearer)? When it comes to dahlia breeding, anything is possible—to an extent. In some respects it's all about picking the right parents and hoping for the best from the dahlia genetic lottery. However, there are a few helpful professional tips worth knowing. The first tip to remember is most dahlia cultivars are octoploids, and therefore already have a crazy number of genes and inherent genetic diversity. It's not always necessary to shake things up too much to produce something quite different. Often the best way to breed new dahlias is to cross those of the same general type. So cross like with like—cactus types with cactus types, single types with other single types, and so forth. Choose a flower type and stick to it.

The second tip has to do with colour. In studies where every seedling plant has been grown and photographed in flower, some breeders have found that most have petals in similar hues to the seed parent, Dahlia Mum. So if you want a tangerine orange dahlia, make sure Dahlia Mum is a pleasing strong shade of orange too.

This seed pod has turned the colour of straw and is now mature and ready for harvest.

The third tip concerns hand pollination versus natural pollination. Our natural pollinators, particularly many species of bees and hoverflies, are exceptional pollinators of dahlias. They do a great job of visiting the tiny florets that make up the dahlia flower as they mature over time. Some breeders like to leave it to the bees and make sure that they grow only dahlia plants with carefully selected characteristics across their plot to lessen the chances of pollen from an undesirable male entering their patch. Others go a step further and isolate the plants in a specific area so that the bees can cross only the selected varieties. They plant the seed-bearing Dahlia Mum among a range of approved pollen-bearing Dahlia Dads, then let nature take its course. This is great for single and semi-double types of flowers, collerettes, and star and single orchid dahlias. However, some types of dahlia flowers, such as pompons and giant decorative blooms, are essentially dense spheres of endless petals. It's not easy for pollinators to get past the layers of petals to the base of the tiny individual florets, where all the pollen is and where fertilization takes place. For these more tightly packed blooms, breeders cut the petals carefully from the flower without removing the stamens and stigmas at the base of the florets. This practice allows for hand-pollination using a paintbrush dusted with pollen from Dahlia Dad.

When seed pods form on the Dahlia Mum, it's best to leave them on the plant for at least four to five weeks until they've matured and started to dry out. At this stage you can harvest them and begin the drying-out process. Dahlia seed is best stored in a dry, cool, frost-free place. I label it and place it in a small paper envelope inside an airtight container, then pop it in the fridge until midspring.

and how floriferous they are. The main characteristics are consistent, though. In a dwarf pompon mixture, for example, all the plants will be short and bushy and the flowers pompon in structure. Sometimes you can find a specific plant in a mixture that you really admire. You can effectively clone it by lifting and saving the tuber and propagating it by taking cuttings and increasing your stocks the following year.

Growing from seed is easy as long as you follow a few key points. Dahlia seeds need a warm temperature of about 18° to 21°C (65–70°F) for good germination. I sow from mid- to late spring, under glass in my lean-to greenhouse, to give myself enough time to grow the plants big enough for planting out in early summer. To get the very best from their dahlia seed and to maximize the germination rate, some breeders and professional growers place seeds in the fridge for about a month before sowing. They also individually feel and check each seed to make sure that it's firm and healthy and use only top-quality compost. Seeds are strictly spaced out in neat rows to allow each seed the very best opportunity for developing with no competition from neighbouring seed. Once pricked out and established, plants are ideally grown on at a cooler temperature of around 10° to 12°C (50–54°F), although they must be kept frost free. At warmer temperatures, plants can grow too quickly and become too tall, soft, and leggy.

Dahlias long to be picked and adored in a vase.

Dahlia seeds are quite large and easy to see, handle, and space on top of the compost. Young seedling plants have healthy appetites, so a good quality brand of general-purpose compost is best; there is no need to fuss with delicate seed compost. Dahlias will soon use up all available nutrients and be shouting for their first feed. I sow dahlias with 2.5 cm (1 in.) between each seed, in a traditional seed tray or into individual modules in a cell pack. Sowing straight into individual small 8 cm (3 in.) pots works well too, as does sowing more densely into a seed pot followed by early pricking out. However, I find the less root disturbance a plant goes through in its first few weeks, the stronger it will establish. Dahlia seeds are fast to germinate and the roots develop quickly, so the slightly deeper seed trays work best. If you've spaced the seeds thinly enough, you can leave them until the first true leaves touch before you pot them up.

In my experience, a little perlite, vermiculite, sand, or fine grit is useful to open up multi-purpose soil-less compost. A wide range of peat-free multi-purpose organic compost is available, and most types work well, as does traditional John Innes Seed Compost.

I like to cover the seed with sifted compost, fine grit, or vermiculite to a depth of about 5 mm (1⁄4 in.). I prefer to soak the tray in a water bath, but you can gently irrigate using a traditional watering can with a fine rose. Be very careful not to wash out any seed or compost. Ideally, it's best to have a propagator. Set it to a temperature of 18° to 21°C (65–70°F), place the lid on, position in a light open spot, and after three days check daily for signs of germination. Once the majority of the seed has emerged, move the tray out of the propagator.

I don't use a propagator because my small lean-to greenhouse is on a southwest-facing wall, and by midspring I can just put my trays inside a clear polyethene bag with a few holes for ventilation, and with this extra protection the heat inside is enough to germinate

A bucket of multi-coloured dahlia blooms. Fully double, multi-petalled forms like decoratives, cactus, and semi-cactus last much longer as cut flowers.

my dahlia seed within two to three weeks. I keep a close eye on night-time temperatures, however, and have a small greenhouse heater on stand-by when chilly spring nights are forecast. I haven't always had the luxury of my greenhouse, but I have raised many successful clutches of dahlia seedlings from trays set inside clear plastic bags on various windowsills around the house. The south-facing kitchen sill always proves to be the quickest.

Ideally, once the first seedling leaves are about 2 cm (0.8 in.) in length, it's time to prick them out. I sow my seed quite thinly, and often wait until individual pairs of true leaves are present and almost touching in their trays. Then I prick out and pot up. I'm usually slightly behind with this task, as it never ceases to amaze me just how rapid germination is and how quickly dahlia seedlings grow. The root system can be well developed at this point, so handle the seedlings with care and prick out as gently as possible.

Cut Flowers

Dahlias long to be picked and adored in a vase. I'm sure of it. They are the ultimate grow-your-own cut flower. The more you cut them, the more flowers they seem to produce. I sometimes wish I had a bigger garden with room for an extra bed devoted to dahlias just for picking. I also wish I still had the time to tend an allotment, but I don't. Neither of these facts stops me from cutting my dahlias throughout the blooming season and enjoying them in the home from the beginning of summer well into autumn.

By cutting a handful of blooms from the garden every few days, you are, in effect, dead-heading a little earlier than normal. Snip just two or three just-opened blooms from each plant. There are often so many buds about to burst into bloom that they'll rarely be missed, and you won't spoil your garden display.

Dahlia Wedding

DAHLIAS ARE FANTASTIC flowers to use in all styles of wedding floristry. You might think their relatively soft, hollow stems would make them unsuitable candidates, but most wedding flowers are wired into place, so this is not an issue. Obvious varieties to grow for weddings are, of course, white and pale cream ones. However, as wedding trends and fashions evolve and change, all sorts of colours are becoming popular. For my friend Amy's wedding, I grew a range of very strong-coloured varieties in deep, dark shades. No whites, creams, or pastels were entertained. Amy wanted to make bold and colourful contrasts by using the incredibly rich dahlia blooms and other exotic flowers in beautiful vintage glass vases along the centre of her long wedding dining table. She also chose to feature random blooms in her bouquet and in buttonholes.

If you are going to grow dahlias for a wedding, be sure to have multiple plants in the varieties you need. Always have extras and backups, and make sure the date of the wedding falls when dahlias are in full bloom. Any time from midsummer into early autumn is a good bet. Growing dahlias for a friend's or family member's wedding makes all the floristry so much more meaningful and personal. The whole occasion becomes much more special and unique. (It does help if your friend or family member also happens to be a very talented florist who is happy to make her own floral creations!)

Dahlias and other exotic flowers in vintage glass vases decorate a formal table setting.

This mixed bunch of pinks, purples, and whites uses all sorts of contrasting flowers and foliage to help show off the dahlias in the arrangement.

Recently I've started to see a greater range of dahlias sold as cut blooms. They are seasonal flowers, so summer and autumn is always going to be their time. If you love to buy bunches of dahlias, head to nurseries or to farmers' markets for the greatest range of blooms, often at bargain prices.

A friend of mine has confessed that she loves dahlia flowers, but finds that they don't last much longer than a day, so don't make great cut flowers. At first I was quite surprised by this statement, but it's true. If you don't pick dahlias properly or grow varieties that are good for cutting, they can be short lived in the vase.

Different forms of dahlia last longer than others, so the choice of flower type and variety is important. Long-stemmed cultivars are, obviously, a huge advantage. As a rule, I find that singles and semi-doubles don't last nearly as long as all of the fully double forms. For cutting I particularly like fully double decorative types, stellar, cactus, semi-cactus, waterlilies, balls, and pompons, all of which have so many layers of petals. If those toward the back of the bloom start to look a little shabby, it's easy to quickly pick them over and spruce up each individual bloom. Dahlias won't last as long in the vase as florist favourites like chrysanthemums, carnations, or alstroemerias. But there are some tips and techniques for cutting that can help you get a good five to seven days out of your cut blooms.

Cut dahlias either early in the morning or late in the evening—essentially, when the sun is at its lowest point and the plant is under as little water stress as possible. Water is absolutely key with cut dahlias. When you cut them, always have handy a bucket or a jug at least half full of water so you can quickly plunge in the cut stems. Don't ever cut dahlias and put them in a trug (a wooden basket), like you would roses or other garden flowers. Dahlias are very thirsty, and the flow of water up the stem is crucial. After a bloom has been cut, it will keep developing and increase in size if water uptake is good.

Always use a sharp knife or very sharp florist's scissors and, ideally, make a diagonal cut so the surface area in contact with the water is as big as possible. Most dahlias have quite hollow stems, so trapped air can block the uptake of water and cause prematurely droopy blooms. Use a sharp knife to pierce the stem under water about one-third of the way up from the base. You should see little air bubbles as trapped air is released.

Be sure to place to your cut dahlias in spotlessly clean containers, and change the water and re-trim the cut end of the stem every day. In other words, do as much as you can to keep things fresh and ensure that water flows toward the bloom. If you follow all these tips, you should find that your cut dahlias last longer in the vase.

With some bits of autumnal foliage, a few berries, and the odd garden alstromeria, even a very random assortment of dahlias can look stunning.

Dahlias can be used to brighten up and enhance all sorts of areas in the home.

Of Jugs and Jam Jars: Ten-Minute Dahlia Displays

IF YOU GROW dahlias in the garden, it's a shame not to pick a few and enjoy them inside as well. I'm not a trained florist or even an amateur flower arranger, so if I can make floral displays that impress my friends and family, you certainly can too. Dahlias look amazing in any container, and can transform everyday, cheap-as-chips jam jars or tin cans into things of real beauty.

On a day-to-day basis I keep it very quick and simple. First, pick a tin can, vase, jam jar, or jug—nearly any container will do. Study its shape and form. If it's a coloured container, think about what colour range of flowers will either complement or contrast well with it. Opposite colours like reds and greens, oranges and blues, or yellows and purples all contrast well. Grouping together deeper darker shades with brighter ones of the same hue works well too. For example, deep blood red with bright scarlet red, or dark magenta pink with hot lipstick pink. Even more simple is to choose just a single colour and stick to it, but with dahlias it's often more fun to break a few rules. Just have fun. You have my permission to rip up the rule book and clash canary yellow with hot pink.

Fill your container halfway with water. Head into your garden with the container and a pair of sharp scissors. Choose your favourite bits of foliage, interesting-shaped sprigs, unusual leaves—whatever grabs your attention. Allow yourself 10 minutes maximum to collect what you need, and remember that odd numbers of things are always good. Be careful with the scissors, as one false snip can ruin any plant. Take just what you need, and preferably a piece that needs a trim or a stem that won't be missed from the back. If you grow lots of dahlias and have a good range of plants in your garden, it's hard to tell where you've been with your scissors. You don't need many blooms to make a big impact so you won't spoil your garden display one bit.

ARRANGING BOUQUETS AND DISPLAYS

Everyone has a personal view on how best to put together a great dahlia flower arrangement. For me, it's more about colours than anything else. Put together colours and forms of dahlias that contrast and complement each other well, then add a cast of great supporting characters in the form of other flowers. Your foliage will then be your inspiring scenery among which your flowery cast performs. If you get the colours and ingredients right, a home-made, hand-tied bouquet can look just as good, if not better, than a more formally arranged florist version.

For the scenery you may want just one good foliage plant or a green flowering plant. However, for something fuller, with more depth and dimension, choose two or three types of foliage. I like to select from green and bronze fennel flower heads like *Foeniculum vulgare* 'Giant Bronze' and *Bupleurum rotundifolium* 'Griffithii', all sorts of euphorbia (always sear the cut ends with boiling water), dill, corn parsley, lady's mantle, and occasionally long lengths of an ivy called *Hedera helix* 'Plume d'Or'. In early autumn, branches of normally quite dull foliage start to turn stunning shades of gold and bronze for just a few weeks right before the end of the dahlia season. Grab them while you can.

For extra floral dimension, consider different groups of flowers that are in total contrast to dahlias in terms of their flower form and structure, such as larkspurs, alstroemerias, cerinthes, gladioli, or lysimachias. Tall spikes are always good, as are umbel shapes and frothy panicles. If attempting a hand-tied dahlia arrangement fills you with dread, don't despair. Be proud of your home-grown dahlias, and keep it simple. You and your dahlias don't need to worry.

For the easiest type of arrangement, simply cut a good handful of stems from your favourite dahlia varieties. Pick one type of foliage, and cut about 10 stems. Start with a stem of foliage and then add three different dahlias, each a different colour. Add another stem of foliage and another three different coloured dahlias. Keep turning the bunch in your hand, and stop when the bunch feels like it's approaching the size you want. Finally, add a final few stems of foliage, tie off tightly, and trim the ends to fit the container. Voilà. You're done.

If you decide to throw in an odd garden flower with your dahlias, or a few stems of berries or seedheads, you still can't go wrong. The great thing about dahlias is that they do all the work for you.

Most cut dahlia blooms float well on water. This offers up some creative opportunities for using flowers to decorate on special occasions and at summer parties. You can also float blooms in clear glass containers as an alternative to the traditional cut flower stems in a vase. They can transform a children's paddling pool into a floating flower garden, or a simple bowl into a mini centrepiece. It really couldn't be easier, and just a few blooms with mini floating candles can look special.

Most dahlia blooms will float on water. What could be an easier way to display them?

WHERE TO BUY

When planning a visit to any of the locations listed, always check the website for up-to-date information. A few of those listed are nurseries who trade only via their website or at flower shows and prefer not to receive visitors.

CANADA

Ferncliff Gardens
8502 McTaggart Street
Mission, British Columbia V2V 6S6
www.ferncliffgardens.com

FGL Dahlias
688 Charbonneau
Saint-Lazare, Québec J7T 2B3
www.fgldahlias.com

UNITED KINGDOM

Abacus Nurseries
Drummau Road
Skewen, Neath
West Glamorgan
Scotland SA10 6NW
www.abacus-nurseries.co.uk

Avon Bulbs
Burnt House Farm
Mid Lambrook
South Petherton
Somerset
England TA13 5HE
www.avonbulbs.co.uk

Aylett Nurseries
North Orbital Road
St Albans
Hertfordshire
England AL2 1DH
www.aylettnurseries.co.uk

Ball Colegrave Trial Ground
Milton Road
West Adderbury
Banbury
Oxfordshire
England OX17 3EY
www.ballcolegrave.co.uk

Bridgemere Nurseries
Nantwich
Cheshire
England CW5 7QB
www.thegardencentregroup.co.uk/garden-centres/bridgemere/Bridgemere-Nursery-and-Garden-World/2

Cotswold Garden Flowers
Sands Lane
Badsey
Evesham
Worcestershire
England WR11 7EZ
www.cgf.net

Great Dixter House and Gardens
Northiam
Rye
East Sussex
England TN31 6PH
www.greatdixter.co.uk

Halls of Heddon
West Heddon Nursery Centre
Heddon on the Wall
Newcastle upon Tyne
England NE15 0JS
www.hallsofheddon.co.uk

Hardy's Cottage Garden Plants
Priory Lane Nursery
Freefolk Priors
Whitchurch
Hampshire
England RG28 7NJ
www.hardys-plants.co.uk

J.R.G. (Jack Gott Dahlias)
22 Summerville Road
Milnthorpe
Cumbria
England LA7 7DF
www.jrg-dahlias.co.uk

National Collection of Dahlias
Varfell Farm
Long Rock
Penzance
Cornwall
England TR20 8AQ
www.national-dahlia-collection.co.uk

Ridgeview Nursery
J & I Cruickshanks
Crossroads
Longridge
West Lothian
Scotland EH47 9AB
www.ridgeviewnursery.co.uk

Rose Cottage Plants
Bay Tree Farm
Epping Green
Essex
England CM16 6PU
www.rosecottageplants.co.uk

The Royal Horticultural Society Garden
Wisley
Woking
Surrey
England GU23 6QB
www.rhs.org.uk/Gardens/Wisley

Ryecroft Dahlias
21 Spierbridge Road
Storrington
West Sussex
England RH20 4PG
ryecroftdahlias.co.uk

Sarah Raven's Garden and Cookery School
Perch Hill Farm
Brightling
Robertsbridge
East Sussex
England TN32 5HP
www.sarahraven.com

Station House Nurseries
Station Road
Burton, Neston
South Wirral
Cheshire
England CH64 5SD
www.eurodahlia.com

Walkers Bulbs
Washway House Farm
Washway Road
Holbeach
Spalding
England PE12 7PP
www.bulbs.co.uk

Withypitts Dahlias
Turners Hill
West Sussex
England RH10 4SF.
www.withypitts-dahlias.co.uk

Worlds End Nurseries
Moseley Road
Hallow
Worcester
England WR2 6NJ
www.worldsendgarden.co.uk

UNITED STATES

Alpen Gardens
12010 NE Flett Road
Gaston, Oregon 97119
www.alpengardens.com

Alpha Dahlias
1101 Campmeeting Road
Sewickley, Pennsylvania 15143
www.alphadahlias.com

Arrowhead Dahlias
404 Elizabeth Avenue
Platteville, Colorado 80651
www.dahlias.net/htmbox/arrowhead.htm

Aztec Dahlias
2115 Adobe Road
Petaluma, California 94954
www.aztecdahlias.com

B and D Dahlias
19857 Marine View Drive SW
Normandy Park, Washington 98166
www.bddahlias.com

Betty's Amazing Dahlias
23858 SE 216th Street
Maple Valley, Washington 98038
www.bettysamazingdahlias.com

Birch Bay Dahlias
12027 62nd Avenue South
Seattle, Washington 98178
www.birchbaydahlias.com/page6.html

Corralitos Gardens
296 Browns Valley Road
Corralitos, California 95076
cgdahlias.com/index.html

Cowlitz River Dahlias
100 Chapman Road
Castle Rock, Washington 98611
www.dahlias4u.com

Dahlia Barn
13110 446th Avenue SE
North Bend, Washington 98045
www.dahliabarn.com

Dahlia Hill
1320 West Main Street
Midland, Michigan 48640
www.dahliahill.org

Dahlias by Les and Viv Connell
6407 119th Avenue East
Puyallup, Washington 98390
www.dahliasbylesandviv.com

Dan's Dahlias
994 South Bank Road
Oakville, Washington 98568
www.dansdahlias.com

Endless Summer Flower Farm
57 East Fork Road
Camden, Maine 04843
www.endlesssummerflowerfarm.com

Frey's Dahlias
12054 Brick Road SE
Turner, Oregon 97392
www.freysdahlias.com

Hamilton Dahlia Farm
47th Street
Hamilton, Michigan 49419
www.hamiltondahliafarm.com

Hollyhill Dahlias
18283 Holly Lane
Oregon City, Oregon 97045
www.hollyhilldahlias.com

Homestead Dahlias
8440 Rice Valley Road
Yoncalla, Oregon 97499
www.dahlias.net/htmbox/homesteaddahlias.htm

J and C Dahlias
3822, 163rd Street East
Tacoma, Washington 98446
www.jcdahlias.com

Jan's Country Garden
344 O'Brien Road
Port Angeles, Washington 98362
www.janscountrygarden.com

Linda's Dahlias
1525 SE Washougal River Road
Washougal, Washington 98671
www.lindasdahlias.com

Lobaugh's Dahlias
113 Ramsey Road
Chehalis, Washington 98532
www.lobaughsdahlias.com

Love House Dahlias
7922 Santa Ana Road
Ventura, California 93001
www.lovehousedahlias.com

Lynch Creek Farm Dahlias
2051 SE Lynch Road
Shelton, Washington 98584
www.lynchcreekdahlias.com

Mingus Dahlias
7407 NE 139th Street
Vancouver, Washington 98662
www.dahlias.net/htmbox/MingusDahlias.htm

Mohawk Dahlia Gardens
92859 Saddleview Drive
Marcola, Oregon 97454
www.dahlias.net/htmbox/mohawk.htm

Old House Dahlias
8005 SE Mill Street
Portland, Oregon 97215
www.oldhousedahlias.com

Parks Dahlias
661 Starveout Creek Road
Azalea, Oregon 97410
www.cruger.com/pkdahlia.html

Sea-Tac Dahlia Gardens
20020 Des Moines Memorial Drive
Seattle, Washington 98198
www.sea-tacgardens.com

Swan Island Dahlias
995 NW 22nd Avenue
Canby, Oregon 97013
www.dahlias.com

Verrone's Pride of the Prairie Dahlias
8925 Burnett Road SE
Yelm, Washington 98597
www.wadahlias.com

Woodland's Dahlias
37003 NW Pacific Highway
Woodland, Washington 98674
www.dahlias.net/htmbox/woodlandsdahlias.htm

Wynne's Dahlias
1395 Willeys Lake Road
Ferndale, Washington 98248
www.wynnesdahlias.com

WHERE TO SEE

When planning a visit to any of the locations listed, always check the website for up-to-date information, especially opening times. Some of the parks, gardens, and trial grounds listed are open to the public only on particular dates during dahlia blooming season. Some locations may require you to make a special appointment.

UNITED KINGDOM

Anglesey Abbey
Quy Road
Lode
Cambridge
England CB25 9EJ
www.nationaltrust.org.uk/anglesey-abbey

Biddulph Grange Garden
Grange Road
Biddulph
Staffordshire
England ST8 7SD
www.nationaltrust.org.uk/biddulph-grange-garden

Chatsworth House
Chatsworth
Bakewell
Derbyshire
England DE45 1PP
www.chatsworth.org

Chenies Manor
The Manor House
Chenies
Buckinghamshire
England WD3 6ER
www.cheniesmanorhouse.co.uk

Great Dixter House and Gardens
Northiam
Rye
East Sussex
England TN31 6PH
www.greatdixter.co.uk

Hever Castle and Gardens
Hever
Edenbridge
Kent
England TN8 7NG
www.hevercastle.co.uk

Kelmarsh Hall and Gardens
Kelmarsh
Northamptonshire
England NN6 9LY
www.kelmarsh.com

National Dahlia Society
Exhibition Trial Ground
Golden Acre Park
Arthington Lane
Bramhope
Leeds
West Yorkshire
England LS16 8BQ
www.leeds.gov.uk/leisure/Pages/Golden-Acre-Park.aspx

Nymans
Handcross
Haywards Heath
Sussex
England RH17 6EB
www.nationaltrust.org.uk/nymans

Poppy Cottage
Ruan High Lanes
Truro
Cornwall
England TR2 5JR
www.poppycottagegarden.co.uk

Rousham House and Gardens
Steeple Aston
Bicester
Oxfordshire
England OX25 4QU
www.rousham.org

The Royal Horticultural Society Garden
Wisley
Woking
Surrey
England GU23 6QB
www.rhs.org.uk/Gardens/Wisley

The Secret Gardens of Sandwich
The Salutation
Knightrider Street
Sandwich
Kent
England CT13 9EW
www.the-secretgardens.co.uk

Valley Gardens
Valley Drive
Harrogate
Yorkshire
England HG2 0QB
www.harrogate.gov.uk/pos/Pages/ValleyGardens.aspx

UNITED STATES

American Dahlia Society
Canby Oregon Trial Garden
995 NW 22nd Avenue
Canby, Oregon 97013
www.dahlias.com

American Dahlia Society
Eastern Trial Garden
Mid Island Dahlia Society
Eisenhower Park
1899 Hempstead Turnpike Entrance
East Meadow, New York 11554
www.midislanddahlia.com/etgarden.html

American Dahlia Society
Great Smoky Mountains Trial Garden
The Village Green Park
US 64 and NC 107
Cashiers, North Carolina 28717
www.villagegreencashiersnc.com/dahlias.htm

American Dahlia Society
Inland Empire Dahlia Trial Garden
Manito Park and Botanical Gardens
4 West 21st Avenue
Spokane, Washington 99203
www.manitogardens.com

American Dahlia Society
Midwest Dahlia Trial Garden
Bonneyville Mill County Park
53373 County Road 131
Bristol, Indiana 46507
www.midwestdahliaconference.org

American Dahlia Society
Pacific Northwest Trial Garden
Point Defiance Park
5400 North Pearl Street
Tacoma, Washington 98407
www.metroparkstacoma.org/point-defiance-park

Bellevue Botanical Garden
12001 Main Street
Bellevue, Washington 98005
www.bellevuebotanical.org/dahlia.html

Dahlia Dell, Conservatory of Flowers
Golden Gate Park
100 John F Kennedy Drive
San Francisco, California 94118
www.conservatoryofflowers.org

Dahlia Society of Georgia
Dahlia Display Garden
U.S. Highway 78 East, Exit 8
Stone Mountain, Georgia 30087
www.dahliasocietyofgeorgia.com

Long Island Dahlia Society Dahlia Garden
Bayard Cutting Arboretum
440 Montauk Highway
Great River, New York 11739
www.bayardcuttingarboretum.com

Mendocino Coast Botanical Gardens
18220 North Highway One
Fort Bragg, California 95437
www.gardenbythesea.org

Puget Sound Dahlia Association
Dahlia Display Garden, Volunteer Park
1400 East Galer Street, Capitol Hill
Seattle, Washington 98112
www.pugetsounddahlias.org

Shore Acres State Park
89814 Cape Arago Highway
Coos Bay, Oregon 97420
www.shoreacres.net/index.php/about-us/shore-acres-state-park

South Coast Botanic Garden
26300 Crenshaw Boulevard
Palos Verdes Peninsula, California 90274
www.southcoastbotanicgarden.org

FOR MORE INFORMATION

BOOKS

Christopher, Marina. 2006. *Late Summer Flowers*. London, England: Frances Lincoln.

Collins, Ted. 2003. *Dahlias: A Colour Guide*. Marlborough, Wiltshire, England: The Crowood Press.

Collins, Ted. 2001. *The New Plant Library: Dahlias*. London, England: Anness Publishing.

Drew, Sue. 2009. *RHS Plant Trials Bulletin: Open-centred Dahlias*. Wisley, Surrey, England: Royal Horticultural Society.

Gillman, Jeff. 2008. *The Truth About Garden Remedies*. Portland, Oregon: Timber Press.

Gillman, Jeff. 2008. *The Truth About Organic Gardening*. Portland, Oregon: Timber Press.

Holland, Wayne. 1996. 'Color Mutations in the Dahlia' in *Dahlias of Today 1996*. Puget Sound, Washington: Puget Sound Dahlia Association.

Lloyd, Christopher. 2001. *Christopher Lloyd's Garden Flowers*. London, England: Cassell.

McClaren, Bill. 2004. *Encyclopedia of Dahlias*. Portland, Oregon: Timber Press.

National Dahlia Society. 2010. *How to Grow Dahlias for the Garden and for Showing*. Aldershot, Hampshire, England: National Dahlia Society.

National Dahlia Society. 2010. *Raising Dahlias from Seed*. Aldershot, Hampshire, England: National Dahlia Society.

Ogg, Stuart. 1961. *Dahlias: A Penguin Handbook*. London, England: Penguin Books.

Rowlands, Gareth. 1999. *The Gardener's Guide to Growing Dahlias*. Newton Abbot, Devon, England: David and Charles.

Thrower, Percy. 1967. *Percy Thrower's Practical Guides: Dahlias and Chrysanthemums*. London, England: W. H. and L. Collingridge.

Unwin, Chas. W. J. 1956. *Gladioli and Dahlias*. London, England: W. H. and L. Collingridge.

Welling, Eleanor. 2007. *The Dahlia Primer: Little Known Facts About the Dahlia*. Bloomington, Indiana: Xlibris Corporation.

WEBSITES

Charity Dahlias: www.kesdahlias.co.uk. Created by dahlia expert and enthusiast Ken Stock.

Dahlia France Forum: dahlia.france.free.fr

Dahlia Suppliers: dahliasuppliers.com

Dahlia World: www.dahliaworld.co.uk. Managed by dahlia expert and enthusiast Dave Bates.

Keith Hammett: www.drkeithhammett.co.nz. Run by a professional plant breeder and plant scientist.

Scottish Dahlia Scene: www.dahlias.co.uk

Stanford Dahlia Project: www.stanford.edu

Wild Dahlias: wilddahlias.com. Created by Dahlia species expert Dayle E. Saar.

ORGANIZATIONS

American Dahlia Society: www.dahlias.org

Canadian Chrysanthemum and Dahlia Society: www.mumsanddahlias.com

Danish Dahlia Society: www.danskdahlia.dk

German Dahlia, Fuchsia and Gladioli Society: www.ddfgg.de

German Dahlia Society: www.dahlie.net

Japan Dahlia Society: www.dahliakai.com/profile.html

National Dahlia Society of United Kingdom: www.dahlia-nds.co.uk

New Zealand Dahlia Society: www.nzdahliasociety.50megs.com

HARDINESS ZONE TEMPERATURES

USDA ZONES & CORRESPONDING TEMPERATURES

Temp °F			Zone	Temp°C		
-60	to	-55	1a	-51	to	-48
-55	to	-50	1b	-48	to	-46
-50	to	-45	2a	-46	to	-43
-45	to	-40	2b	-43	to	-40
-40	to	-35	3a	-40	to	-37
-35	to	-30	3b	-37	to	-34
-30	to	-25	4a	-34	to	-32
-25	to	-20	4b	-32	to	-29
-20	to	-15	5a	-29	to	-26
-15	to	-10	5b	-26	to	-23
-10	to	-5	6a	-23	to	-21
-5	to	0	6b	-21	to	-18
0	to	5	7a	-18	to	-15
5	to	10	7b	-15	to	-12
10	to	15	8a	-12	to	-9
15	to	20	8b	-9	to	-7
20	to	25	9a	-7	to	-4
25	to	30	9b	-4	to	-1
30	to	35	10a	-1	to	2
35	to	40	10b	2	to	4
40	to	45	11a	4	to	7
45	to	50	11b	7	to	10
50	to	55	12a	10	to	13
55	to	60	12b	13	to	16
60	to	65	13a	16	to	18
65	to	70	13b	18	to	21

FIND HARDINESS MAPS ON THE INTERNET.

United States *http://www.usna.usda.gov/Hardzone/ushzmap.html*

Canada *http://www.planthardiness.gc.ca/* or *http://atlas.nrcan.gc.ca/site/english/maps/environment/forest/forestcanada/planthardi*

Europe *http://www.gardenweb.com/zones/europe/* or *http://www.uk.gardenweb.com/forums/zones/hze.html*

ACKNOWLEDGEMENTS

This book is dedicated to my granddad, Arthur Worrall, who introduced me to dahlias and passed on a love of gardening, and also to my dad, who gave me the best advice a father ever could: "Do a job that you love."

I must offer a huge amount of thanks to a number of friends, florists, horticulturists, and dahlia experts who have helped to keep the fires of my dahlia passion burning bright. When it comes to highly advanced and international dahlia matters, I am privileged to be able to confide in Royal Horticultural Society judge, ex-National Dahlia Society president, and all-around dahlia superstar Jon Wheatley. For friendship, advice, and consultations on dahlia varieties I also thank my dahlia colour guru, Sarah Raven.

At the National Collection of Dahlias in Cornwall, Mike Mann and Mark Twyning have been hugely supportive and happy to help with any queries and questions.

Very special thanks must go to Darren Share, the Head of Birmingham City Parks and Nurseries, and the staff at Kings Heath Park and Cofton Nurseries. They have enabled me to grow more dahlia varieties than my small garden ever could have contained, and I am indebted to them for their enthusiastic collaboration. Thanks to Chris Brown, Tony Turpin, Andi Jennings, Wendy Pitkin, Alison Green, and Dave Barry.

Finally, love and thanks to my most wonderful friend Rosemary Edwards for guidance with style, grammar, and punctuation, as well as to my partner, Matthew. Here's to more dahlia adventures around the globe.

PHOTO CREDITS

Photographs are by the author unless indicated otherwise.

EMMA CASE, pages 228–229.
BALL COLEGRAVE, pages 189 left and right, 190 top and middle, and 191 left.
JASON INGRAM, page 252 left.
MATTHEW KIDD, page 252 right.
MARK TWYNING, pages 56 top left, 73 top right, 92 left, 215, and 219.

INDEX

ABOUT THE AUTHOR

ANDY VERNON is a writer, photographer, and television producer-director based in Birmingham, England. His love of dahlias dates back to his earliest formative years, when he spent time on his granddad's allotment among rows of floriferous plants. In his own garden Andy incorporates dahlias into every available planting opportunity, and encourages friends, family, and his local parks department to grow lots of these flamboyant flowers.

Andy has been the producer-director and the series producer of many popular gardening television programmes for the BBC. He studied horticulture at Nottingham University, and trained with the Royal Horticultural Society at Wisley and the Royal Botanic Gardens at Kew. He has also worked in gardens and parks in the Cayman Islands, Cuba, and Miami, Florida, and on the island of Kauai.

At home, Andy can often be found in his greenhouse propagating lots of his beloved dahlias. You can also encounter him behind a camera, taking photographs, or filming in gardens. In late summer he often visits dahlia locations around the United Kingdom with his partner, Matt, and his beloved Jack Russells Daisy, Percy, and Lulu. Catch up with Andy at www.planetdahlia.co.uk.

Front cover: 'Jitterbug'
Spine: 'Mrs McDonald Quill'
Title page: 'Boogie Nites'
Contents page: 'Hallwood Satin'

Published in 2014 by Timber Press, Inc.

The Haseltine Building
133 S.W. Second Avenue, Suite 450
Portland, Oregon 97204-3527

6a Lonsdale Road
London NW6 6RD

For details on other Timber Press books and to sign up for our newsletters, please visit our websites, timberpress.com and timberpress.co.uk.

Library of Congress Cataloging-in-Publication Data
Vernon, Andy.
The plant lover's guide to dahlias/Andy Vernon.—1st ed.
p. cm.
Includes index.
ISBN 978-1-60469-416-1
1. Dahlias. I. Title.
SB413.D13V47 2014
635.9'3399—dc23 2013029156

A catalogue record for this book is also available from the British Library.

Book and cover design by Laken Wright
Printed in China

THE **PLANT LOVER'S GUIDE** TO

SALVIAS

JOHN WHITTLESEY

THE **PLANT LOVER'S GUIDE** TO

BRENT HORVATH

THE **PLANT LOVER'S GUIDE** TO

SNOWDROPS

NAOMI SLADE